H.J. Heinz Company
600 Grant Street
Pittsburgh
Pennsylvania

.y 1991

I must admit that by the time of my last cap, in 1971 at the age of 34, I was some way from my peak. As Willie John McBride said, "O'Reilly, your best attacking move today will be to shake your jowls at your opposite number."

Rugby has always been more than a game for me. It was a great voyage of self-discovery, a great tutorial, a template for life. I started at 18 years of age, four years younger than anyone on the British Lions team that toured South Africa in 1955. I travelled all over the world playing Rugby. My travels taught me that this world is full of different cultural norms but that people are also very similar.

In all, I was honoured to win 10 caps for the Lions as well as 29 for Ireland and my love of Rugby has never waned. I'm therefore delighted that Heinz in the UK has decided to sign up and sponsor the greatest Rugby tournament in the world.

I know that the British arm of Heinz is planning to associate the company with the ideals and values of Rugby Football. Values of equality, of health and fitness, of teamwork. And damn good fellowship after the game.

See you there.

TONY O'REILLY.

Win a five-star package for two to see the mighty England play in the Rugby World Cup finals.

Stay in the five-star luxury of the Royal Garden Hotel, the official headquarters for the Rugby World Cup, 1991. Return rail fares to London from anywhere in the United Kingdom will also be provided.

The Royal Garden, owned by Rank Hotels, is uniquely situated on the edge of Hyde Park, adjacent to Kensington Palace. Close to all of the fashionable stores of Knightsbridge, it will be the centre of attraction during the forthcoming Rugby World Cup, accommodating V.I.P.s and officials from all over the world.

Here's how to enter:

Simply study the questions overleaf and, when you think you have the right answer, insert it in the corresponding space. Complete the panel, cut it out and send it to Promotions Business Ltd, 2 Sherland Road, Twickenham, Middlesex TW1 4HD. The closing date for entries is 14 September 1991. The first two correct entries picked out of the hat on the closing date will win two tickets to see England play in the Rugby World Cup finals, return rail fare and an overnight stay at the Royal Garden Hotel.

RULES: The organizer's decision is final and no correspondence will be entered into. Entries must be on a recognized entry form – no photocopies will be accepted. No alternative cash prize will be offered. Entries received after the closing date will be declared null and void.

1. John Jeffrey, the current Scottish international, has also played for which other home country?

2. Who captained the Welsh Triple Crown winning side of 1988?

3. How many times have Scotland won the Grand Slam?

4. Who is the only player to have played in the Pilkington Cup Final one year and in the Schweppes Cup Final the next?

5. Which current New Zealand squad member was also selected to represent his nation at judo in the 1980 olympics?

6. Which current England player has played against France every year since 1984?

7. Who is the only current member of the England squad to have played against all of the International Board member countries including South Africa?

8. Which teams compete of the Bowring Bowl?

9. Which player has scored the most tries for England in a Five Nations Championship season?

10. Who won the 1991 Middlesex Sevens tournament?

ANSWERS

1. ....
2. ....
3. ....
4. ....
5. ....
6. ....
7. ....
8. ....
9. ....
10. ...London Scottish...

NAME ....
ADDRESS ....
....
....
TELEPHONE NUMBER ....

THE DAILY TELEGRAPH RUGBY UNION WORLD CUP GUIDE 1991

Edited by
Chris Jones

Sidgwick & Jackson Limited

CONTENTS

WINNING THE WORLD CUP

by
David Kirk
captain of New Zealand, the 1987 World Cup champions
who defeated France 29–9 in the inaugural final

OPPOSITE AND ABOVE: David Kirk, the
New Zealand captain, scoring one of his
team's tries in the World Cup final of 1987.

The World Cup preparations for each player begin much earlier than most people can be aware. It began for me the moment I walked off the field in the last game of the previous season. Even then, there were training programmes to be thought of, a build-up to be managed that allowed enough fitness and sharpness to ensure selection and yet left enough in reserve for the strains of the month of play. The selection process was relentless: club matches, provincial matches, regional matches, a final trial – always on show, always on edge. There is no secret to winning the World Cup: it is about preparation, selection, training, the ability to withstand pressure and most importantly the will to win. Something the last tournament will have taught many is that once

9

it begins, the successful campaign is the one that builds momentum as it unfolds. Each match is a stepping stone to the next, each game a vital opportunity to improve.

The momentum we were able to build up in 1987 was the key to our success. Italy and Fiji were despatched and the record books re-written at the same time as Sean Fitzpatrick, Michael Jones and John Gallagher were introduced to the world. Argentina provided a chance to ensure all the squad were involved in our campaign and then onto Scotland, our first real test. The euphoria, the easy confidence of the first three victories counted for nothing in the tension of the quarter-final against the best of the Home Nations. But, the desire burned brightly and on we moved to the semi-final. Videos gave us an opportunity to minutely dissect Wales. Their performance in beating England gave us confidence and we went to Brisbane knowing ourselves now, comfortable with our power, aware of our momentum. The match was won inside five minutes and the ultimate prize was there to be taken.

A final bus ride – this time it was more like going home; a final changing-room build-up – the quietest most introspective of the campaign; a final toss and a final kick-off against France. All that was left was eighty minutes. We had done enough to earn our opportunity to prove we were the best in the world, now we had to take it. We were ready. Never before had any of us played in such a team; the explosive power of the forwards and the strength, speed and smoothness of the backs was new, even to New Zealand Rugby.

Without doubt the hardest match of the tournament, it was won fifteen minutes after half-time and from that moment we knew we were to be world champions.

And so finally, there I was, walking up the stairs behind the Main Stand at Eden Park, about to emerge and accept the Cup on behalf of the team, even the country. The roar, the sweet feel of the Cup in my hands, the joy of fulfilling a dream and the relief of the lifting of a burden.

OPPOSITE: *Team work; the key to the All Blacks success. Grant Fox, the goal kicking outside-half, has plenty of support on hand.*

BELOW: *Serge Blanco, the world's most capped player, tries to elude Buck Shelford's tackle in the final.*

THE WORLD CUP STORY

by
Mick Cleary

The comment cut through the thick, smokey air. 'What about a World Cup?'
There was silence, followed by a few sardonic chuckles. 'You'll never get
away with that.' And so began the World Cup. At the time it was no more
than an aside in an International Board committee room: a throw-away line
thought some, a bloody cheek thought others. Conservatism was so deeply-
rooted in many members of the Board that there was no way such a
revolutionary idea could ever come to pass.

It came to pass. Today the World Cup is the focus of every rugby nation in
the world. Of course, there is the little matter of the Five Nations' Championship, the Bledisloe Cup, overseas tours, not to mention the Lions to consider
as well. However, every country, no matter how fixed they might be on
stuffing the living daylights out of next week's opposition, will in fact have
their horizon very much fixed on the next World Cup. The World Cup is the
centre of everyone's thinking: teams plan strategy and personnel in four year
cycles; supporters of the world champions long for their four-years-worth of
gloating, whilst the players themselves have begun to work out their retirement dates according to the same calendar. The World Cup is here to stay.

One might ask why it took so long to arrive in the first place. After all,
soccer, a younger sport than rugby, has been into global action for almost
sixty years. In fact soccer's example was probably one of the main reasons that
rugby dragged its heels for so long. It feared not so much the unknown as the
known. It saw the rampant commercialism of football, it saw a game crucified
by problems of spectator violence, on-the-field tantrums, internal wrangling,

*Buck Shelford refuses to give up possession despite Ieuan Evans' tackle in the one sided
1987 semi-final clash with Wales.*

excessive and usually hostile media interest and so on. It did not want to belong to that little club, thank you very much. The rugby authorities prided themselves on the control they exerted on the game. Open it up to a world competition and goodness knows who might come through the door.

The fears were groundless. Those that have come through the door have shown themselves every bit as worthy in their sporting intentions of sharing the same pitches and committee rooms as the long-established members of the International Board. Indeed one of the great attractions of the whole World Cup venture was the opportunity to draw in the emerging countries and to stimulate the growth of the game around the globe. That at least was the prospect which brought a glint to the eye of the late John Kendall-Carpenter. The English schoolmaster, former international and IB representative, was one of the few who responded positively to the idea when it cut through the smoke and chatter of an International Board meeting one afternoon.

New Zealand and Australia first tossed the idea in and followed it up with a feasibility study in 1984. Their delegates, Dick Littlejohn and Sir

The driving force behind the 1991 World Cup. (left to right) The late John Kendall-Carpenter, Ray Williams and Allan Callan at a press briefing.

Nicholas Shehadie, impressed Kendall-Carpenter with their vision. So much so that Kendall-Carpenter became the first Chairman of the World Cup sub-committee. He lobbied, planned, travelled, cajoled, bullied and went down on bended knee until, at a meeting of the Board held in Paris in March 1985, the brave venture was approved. A typically bland statement recorded the historic moment: 'Following very full discussion, the Board agreed to proceed with the staging of this competition in 1987.'

That was the easy part. Now Kendall-Carpenter had to put the whole thing together. At least he had a fount of goodwill to draw from. 'It'll give us something more to play for, especially if we get into the final stages, because people in the States love a winner,' said Bob Jones of the United States. Bryce Rope from New Zealand was another who gave the tournament a very definite thumbs-up. 'The World Cup will widen the whole scope of the game. Rugby is developing so fast in so many countries like Argentina, Poland and Russia, that you can't stand still.' Monty Heald of Canada voiced the great joy of many of the smaller rugby playing nations when he said: 'The World Cup decision was a good one, particularly for those nations outside the IRB: it gives them the opportunity to get higher competition and puts a bit more pressure on the staid Home Unions to open things up.'

That the 1987 World Cup was something of a hotch-potch is not surprising. It took the modern Olympics almost a century to break even and, although not quite on the same scale, the inaugural World Cup had little time to get its act together. In fact on Kendall-Carpenter's own admission, 'the 1987 World Cup was an experiment.' That comment was made in retrospect, long after the tournament had been completed. When the tournament was first announced, the organisers had no idea who would be participating. With less than two years to go, Kendall-Carpenter was only able to speculate on the final make-up: 'Obviously one area to which we shall be directing our attentions early on, will be the scope that exists for involving all eight of the IB nations and the invitations to be extended to competing countries.'

As it was, sixteen countries were invited: England, Australia, Japan, USA, Canada, Ireland, Tonga, Wales, Argentina, Fiji, Italy, New Zealand, France, Romania, Scotland and Zimbabwe. All the leading countries were there. With one notable exception, South Africa. It was a problem which taxed the diplomatic energies of Kendall-Carpenter in the early days with the threat of a

Robert Jones, the talented Welsh scrum-half, looks for support against Ireland in the 1987 pool game between the teams. Wales triumphed 13–6 in Wellington and went on to the semi-finals.

professional circus in South Africa an ever-present concern. The issue tested his patience and loyalties sorely. Just nine months before the kick-off he commented: 'I have a very protective feeling towards staging the World Cup. Anything which is likely to frustrate that end I shall combat. If one senses that South Africa, because they're denied participation, denigrate the tournament, then I shall of course feel hostile to those people. I would of course have liked to see them participate. It's a competition and therefore merit is essential. Without South Africa that merit is questioned. If they believe in amateur rugby, then they should demonstrate the purity of the ideal and rise above the easy, short-term options. They ought not to knock down other people's castles.'

Kendall-Carpenter's castle survived. Even if the main sponsor, KDD, was rather late in arriving; even if the television contract for the whole tournament was not signed until a few minutes before the kick-off; even if there were numerous logistical cock-ups with tickets; even if . . . The whole thing was a wonderful success if only for the simple reason that it took place.

John Kendall-Carpenter stood behind All Black captain David Kirk as he held aloft the William Webb Ellis trophy at Eden Park, Auckland on 20 June 1987. His mind was already far away. He knew the real test for Rugby's World Cup lay in establishing a competition which would stand the test of time. There had been mistakes, some unavoidable, many not, and Kendall-Carpenter was anxious to put things right. He believed, quite adamantly, that the continuing success of the World Cup was vital for the future of the game.

Of course, there was a slight danger that the International Board themselves might decide to kill off the competition. In theory the 1987 venture was no more than a one-off and any future tournament had to be ratified by the Board. The rubber stamp was duly delivered at the annual meeting in March 1988. By that time the members had studied a ninety-page report submitted by New Zealand and heard several telling comments from those involved in the organisation.

There was one point made by nearly all concerned: the 1991 tournament should be held in one country. The logistical, legal and practical difficulties of staging the event in two countries had severely handicapped the inaugural Cup. And so to the monumental decision reached in London on 25 March 1988: 'The tournament will be under the control of the Board and administered by the Five Nations. Matches will be played in England, Scotland, Ireland, Wales and France.'

Not one, not two, but *five* countries. The noose of compromise seemed once more to be hanging round the neck of rugby. When Albert Ferrasse, Chairman of the Board at the time, cryptically remarked at its interim meeting in Agen in 1987 that, 'For the time being everyone is a candidate and no-one is a candidate,' we should have known that France had little intention of giving up a slice of the action.

Of course France, with its superb stadia, keen regional support, not to mention the best cuisine in the world, was, and always will be, perfectly capable of staging the tournament on its own. The Home Unions had a historical case to plead and the end result . . . fudge. Trying to locate, conduct and implement commercial deals across five countries was always going to be a nightmare, and so it has proven. The commercial side of the World Cup operation has, since the very beginning, been the cause of the biggest headaches and the source of much antagonism.

If only these tournaments were simply about a series of 80-minute nuggets

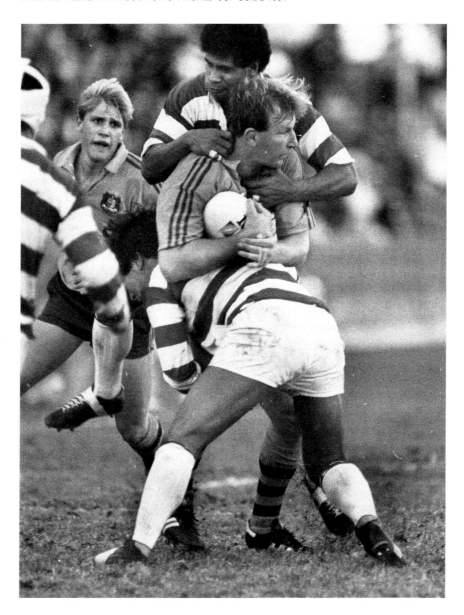

Steve Tuynman, one of Australia's try scorers in a 42–23 World Cup win over Japan. The Japanese won many friends with their refusal to accept defeat and crunching tackling.

of rugby. Everyone would be happy and there would be no wrangling. As it is, money is a key factor. Some were surprised that the 1987 tournament yielded a profit of only $1.95 million (US). Even Dick Littlejohn, who headed the New Zealand administration, admitted that: 'When you consider the scale of the event, a profit of this kind is puny. In years to come, people will laugh at these figures.'

Money was, and very much is, important to the World Cup. Not so that grey-suited accountants could step forward at the end of the event, take a bow and also take a huge slice of the proceeds. Rugby World Cup wanted the money to ensure control of its own destiny. As Kendall–Carpenter noted: 'The success of the second World Cup is vital for the success of the game. We need money to develop the game world wide. We want to look to the game in a world context and support the ambitions of smaller nations. A successful World Cup would increase awareness for the sport and provide the IRB with the means to set up coaching schemes, improve contacts with unions and finally enrich the game in the world.'

Kendall–Carpenter had travelled over 150,000 miles in the two years leading up to the 1987 tournament, and he still held down a full-time job. It was obvious that the World Cup needed professional administrators. The concept was accepted by the IRB and in May 1988 Keith Rowlands became the first full-time professional Secretary. Rowlands was selected from a field of seventy applicants. Even though his brief was rather vague, as well as much broader than just considering the World Cup, there was little doubt that the 1991 tournament was to occupy much of his time. By November he, in consultation with others, had done enough to convince the Board of the need to set up a tournament committee which consisted of himself, Kendall–Carpenter, Marcel Martin (France) and Russ Thomas (New Zealand). These men were to construct the commercial template which they hoped would serve the game for generations to come.

The aim was simply to retain control. Kendall–Carpenter had experienced at first hand in 1987 the difficulties, as well as the disappointments, of dealing with third parties. 'In 1987,' he recalled, 'we went for a firm, West Nally, and for a guarantee. They did the work of going out into the market place and we were assured of $5 million. Well, that was the idea but reality marched haphazardly alongside aspiration. We needed a strong nerve because neither the host broadcaster contract nor any significant sponsorship was clinched by April 1987 – a month before the tournament began.

'Rather than looking hopefully toward the $10 million West Nally confidently assured us would, like the US Cavalry, arrive in the nick of time we settled for the lower sum. Just as well: by the time Italy played New Zealand in the inaugural match our commercial representation was a good $1.5 million adrift. NZTV confirmed the contract for the host broadcaster only half an hour before the kick off. You do not forget such things.'

It had also been one of the original, cherished notions of the organisers that Rugby World Cup would not sell its soul. It wanted money but not at any price. Not at the price of an outside commercial enterprise cheapening the image of the sport, as happened with the Olympics. The answer to both

Doug Wyllie on the attack for Scotland in their 60–21 demolition of Zimbabwe at Wellington. Gavin Hastings, the full-back, converted eight of Scotland's tries.

problems was therefore simple – run the whole show itself. If the 1991 World Cup failed to realise its commercial potential or if it fell prey to outside operators, then it would only have itself to blame. This was the scheme devised by the four man committee and put into effect in the summer of 1988 by Kendall-Carpenter and Keith Rowlands. It meant forgoing the security of a guarantee, but the committee were convinced this was the best way forward: namely, to appoint a broker who would recommend different specialists in the various commercial areas to be rejected or appointed by Rugby World Cup itself.

The broker chosen was the Keith Prowse Agency, officially appointed in February 1989, later to become CPMA (Callan, Palmer, Morgan Associates). 'My brief was simply to achieve a balance between income and exposure,' explained Alan Callan, the Commercial Director. 'Rugby World Cup wanted money but not at any cost. I was there to filter the bids and pass on any recommendations. Initially there were some 140 companies who wanted a slice of the action. These ranged from multinational concerns to tiny concerns who I don't think quite realised just how big the rugby World Cup was.'

Mark McCormack's IMG estimated that the tournament was worth about £9 million. ISL thought it more likely to be in the region of £12 million. These totals, however, were gross and did not take into account the commission, as high as 30 per cent, which the companies would take from that total. Not only would it cost Rugby World Cup a lot of money to hire these people, it would also mean handing over control. It was a non-starter.

And so began a protracted process by which Callan's company sifted through bids from all walks of commercial life. Two key appointments were made within a few months and announced in September 1989 – TSL were brought in as broadcast managers whilst Telemundi were nominated as merchandising agents. TSL in particular was a critical move in the right direction. As Australian representative, Ross Turnbull, remarked after the inaugural event: 'The main lesson this time was very simple: get your world-wide television rights tied up as soon as possible.' The reason for that was simple. Without an audience, no prospective sponsor is going to sign on the dotted line.

TSL set about its task with relish and no little commercial dexterity. By November 1990, the income from TV rights was already $18 million, a return which enabled Callan to confidently predict at that point the 1991 event would make a net profit of £25 million. Such a satisfying yield has been helped by the decision of the committee to establish its financial base outside the UK. Rugby World Cup Limited was created in Douglas, on the Isle of Man, whilst a company, called Rugby World Cup BV, dealing with licensing, was set-up in Rotterdam to take advantage of the Double Tax Treaty and royalty arrangements.

Was rugby always such a complex business? There is little doubt that it needed to be. The World Cup is a massive event in all senses of the word. That the precise details of the financial background should be so intricate and, to most of the rugby population, so tedious, should not detract from the efforts of those, many of whom are still amateurs, to apply themselves so earnestly to the task. There have been problems. There have been criticisms levelled, most noticeably that sponsors were very slow in coming forward. Publicity and communication also come in for a few sharp arrows of criticism from the media. However, it must be remarked that the whole tangled web is still a great improvement on what happened in 1987 and the fact that there has been so much critical attention paid by the UK media is an indication of the status the tournament has achieved.

Of course, the most enjoyable part of the whole operation will be the games and this time there can be no gripes from the rest of the world, South Africa excepted. Whereas entry to the 1987 tournament was reserved for the privileged few, 1991 was open to all thirty-seven members of the International Board. Countries like Israel, Sweden, Korea, Italy and Western Samoa had the chance to win through to the finals.

Ray Williams, the former secretary of the WRU, was appointed tournament director in February 1991. His task was not simple. After all, sorting out pitch, shirt and oranges for the Extra Bs involves a fair amount of phone calls and no end of hassle. By the end of 1989 Williams had got them cracking in Copenhagen in the north, Buenos Aires in the south, Toronto in the west and Rocany, near Prague, in the east. At one point in Czechoslovakia he was told that the home team would be unable to continue in the qualifying competition if they won that afternoon against Portugal. When he asked the reason, Williams was taken to the embassy where 3,000 East Germans were camped, all waiting for exit visas. Visas for rugby players were not high on the list of priorities for the Czech authorities. (Portugal won 15–12, so one headache did not materialise for Williams).

By the time England and New Zealand kick off at Twickenham on 3 October 1991, Williams will have trailed across the equivalent of several continents to ensure that all grounds are in shape, that all the tickets are heading to the right destinations, that the eight qualifiers know where they are headed, that the media are happy (some chance) and that the logistical arrangements for the tournament itself proceed smoothly. Not surprisingly, there have been teething difficulties, not the least involved sorting out the complications of having nineteen centres for the final stages which come under four different legal systems. On another tack in the very first preliminary competition, which took place in Tours, France, in May 1989 and featured Denmark, Sweden, Switzerland and Israel, there were complaints from some that they had received no support from the organisers. 'No-one has helped us,' claimed Jean-Jacques Zander, the mastermind of the event. 'The International Rugby Board supported our project, but they told us there was no money in the kitty for the tournament.'

In some ways it was an understandable complaint but one to which it was virtually impossible to attend. 'There just wasn't the finance available,' said Williams. 'It is also desirable that there should be a large self-help element. Rugby has always been that way and, as it turned out, the Tours tournament succeeded which proved that it could be done. Eventually, however, we do hope to establish an International Rugby Settlement whose aim will be to promote rugby football throughout the world. Part of this will involve the funding of the World Cup for those unions most in need.

'I've often said that this is more than just a competition: that Rugby World Cup 1991 must seize the opportunity to go out and market the game. That is why something like the Message Relay is so important. For example, in Scotland the relay will pass through many areas, such as the Orkneys and Shetland where there is little chance for people to experience rugby at first hand. We must draw the young people into our game if we are to secure its future. That is as important a part of the World Cup as who actually wins the competition.'

In many ways Williams has been working in the dark. The 1987 tournament was far different in scope and content. There has been little precedent for much of what he has been involved in. 'It's too early yet to evaluate whether we have got it right or not,' says Williams. 'What can seem to be going brilliantly at one point can suddenly blow up in your face a few months later. On the other hand, what might have seemed insurmountable at one juncture suddenly turns out wonderfully well.

'What I can say is that it has all been a superb challenge and immensely rewarding. On the rugby side my greatest pleasure has come from seeing the way in which Holland have developed: how they have battled to accept their financial responsibilities; how they have learnt and how their game has prospered. I think that as a direct result of their fine efforts in the World Cup they were immediately awarded a B fixture against Wales where previously they would only have merited a Districts match.'

If the infrastructure for the 1991 Cup is shown to work, then the future of the tournament, and the game itself, is assured. The profit generated will ensure that in future years no team will have to suffer financially to compete. That above all else was the dream of John Kendall-Carpenter. Tragically he died of a heart attack in May 1990.

'John Kendall-Carpenter was a great internationalist,' added Williams. 'Not for him the narrow thinking of many rugby administrators. His contribution to Rugby World Cup and to the game itself was immense. It is just so sad that he won't be around to share in what I am sure will be a great tournament. Its success will be a fitting tribute to his work.'

There are many people who, by kick-off time on 3 October 1991, will have invested huge amounts of time and energy in helping the World Cup pass from being a casual comment to a magnificent sporting reality. And a reality that will last.

The eight teams who qualified by right for the 1991 tournament were: England, Ireland, Scotland, Wales, France, New Zealand, Australia, Fiji. Those teams were seeded after their performances at the 1987 event, but only to ensure that the five host countries were kept apart. The other eight places for the 1991 World Cup were secured through the qualifying tournaments staged in Zimbabwe, Italy, Japan and the Americas. As a result eight countries emerged; Western Samoa, Japan, Zimbabwe, Romania, Italy, Canada, USA and Argentina.

Mick Cleary writes for the *Observer*.

PILKINGTON
the world's
leading
glassmaker

*Sponsors
of the
RFU club
knockout
competition*

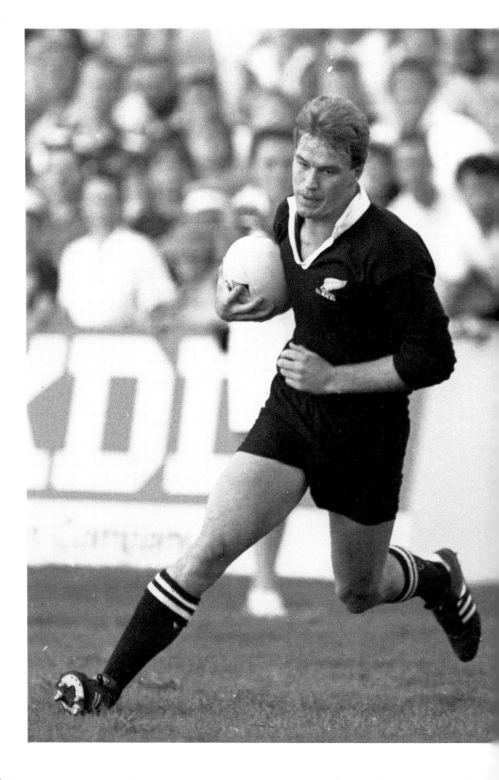

THE SIXTEEN TEAMS COMPETING IN THE 1991 RUGBY UNION WORLD CUP

Group 1

New Zealand (champions)
England
Italy
USA

Group 2

Scotland
Ireland
Japan
Zimbabwe

Group 3

Australia
Wales
Argentina
Western Samoa

Group 4

France
Fiji
Romania
Canada

John Kirwan, the All Black wing, scoring one of his two tries in a 49–6 win over Wales in the semi-final clash at Brisbane. Wales's John Devereux is powerless to stop the try.

*ARGENTINA: The Argentine squad;
they were second in the American qualifying group.*

ARGENTINA

by
Pablo Mamone

The Argentine challenge in the 1991 World Cup has been shaped by its refusal to adopt any changes to rugby's amateur laws. While other countries have welcomed a relaxation in the laws, the Argentinian Rugby Union (UAR) has defended the amateur ethos with real determination, resulting in an exodus of top players to Europe and their exclusion from the national squad. Those players who have opted for the jobs and other benefits offered by French and Italian clubs have automatically banned themselves. It is now a question of how long Argentine rugby can continue to fill the gaps created in the national squad.

The ever-changing face of Argentine rugby was seen on the terribly difficult UK and Ireland tour in 1990 when successive Saturdays provided matches against Ireland, England, Scotland and the Barbarians. Seventeen players new to the high pressure world of international rugby were included in a tour squad captained by Hugo Porta. For nearly two decades Porta has dominated Argentine rugby from outside-half and he will be 40 in September 1991. He still has a vital role to play in his country's rugby future after returning to the top flight following three years self-imposed exile. Porta, who quit international rugby after Argentina's poor showing in the 1987 World Cup, did not share the philosophy of Rodolfo O'Reilly, who was the national coach until the final test of the drawn series (1–1) with England in 1990. When O'Reilly went Porta returned and their conflict was the latest in a long line of powerful arguments that have dominated Argentine rugby. In fighting is par for the course.

Since 1965 the Argentine national side has been known throughout the rugby world as the Pumas. Before starting their first tour outside South

29

Hugo Porta, the hero of Argentine rugby, is caught by Ireland's Brian Smith. Porta has been the dominant figure in his country for nearly two decades.

America, which took them to South Africa, the Argentine squad trained in Rhodesia. A local journalist, impressed with the squad's training performance, wrote comparing them to the puma 'which they have in their coat of arms'. In fact, the animal on the badge is a jaguar but puma stuck.

Angel Guastella helped prepare that 1965 touring team and he was at the centre of a controversy that rocked Puma rugby in 1977. It was to be the first of a whole series of coaching upheavals. The San Isidro Club, under coach Carlos Veco Villegas, devised the 'bajadita' eight man shove in the scrum and this weapon secured sixteen Buenos Aires championships in twenty-two years and a draw with Australia (22–22) in 1987. Villegas coached the Pumas in 1974, 1976 and 1977 but in that year he resigned. The UAR refused to accept the nomination of Arturo Juardo as captain for the South American Cup competition and ten players sided with Villegas. Those players were suspended from Puma rugby for five years. Guastella took over the national team in 1978 and within his camp was Hugo Porta. A major division was created in Argentine rugby between the Villeguistas and the Guastellistas. A tour to the United Kingdom and Italy in 1978 proved to be a major success for Guastella and the Pumas achieved a famous draw with England at Twickenham.

The current coach is Luis Gradin who was in charge of the national team between 1979 and 1981. During this time they enjoyed considerable success touring New Zealand, only losing the test matches, while they accounted for Australia in Buenos Aires. Argentina also claimed a draw at home to England in 1981 and then O'Reilly took over the team and three times he led South American sides (mainly Argentine players) to South Africa.

The coaching job became a major problem again in 1983 with O'Reilly taking Argentina to Australia and a great 18–3 test win in Brisbane and then resigning on his return home. A dispute with his own club caused this situation. Next into the hot seat as coach was Hector Silva and helping with the backs was Angel Guastella. Their team defeated France 24–16 and drew 21–21 with New Zealand. The 1987 World Cup disappointments led to the fall of this duo and back came O'Reilly and a change of fortune earned wins over France and Australia before he finally opted out, for the last time, following the second test win over England in 1990. Yes, it is all very confusing but that is Argentine rugby! Although soccer is the national sport, rugby stirs mighty passions and has existed in Argentina since 1873. From small beginnings the game started to win support and in 1886 the Buenos Aires Rugby and Cricket club was formed, giving the game its first home. Later that year, a match was played between the club and the Rosario Athletic Club and the spread of the game led to the setting up of the River Plate Rugby Union. At the start of this century the Argentine government signed contracts with major British companies and matches between locals and the British later became regular Argentines v Foreigners contests.

Rugby grew apace in Argentina, but during the First World War many of the foreigners had to return to their own countries and the main competition was suspended. In the middle of the war, Club Atletico San Isidro was born and grew into the country's leading club. When the championship resumed in 1919 it was CASI who dominated until 1930. Then, in 1948 a combined Oxford-Cambridge side arrived and initiated a swift growth in Argentine rugby. The UAR (which succeeded the River Plate RU) regarded the matches with Oxbridge as its first 'tests' and the English team triumphed 17–0 and 39–0. Tours by France, Ireland and the Junior Springboks helped improve Argentine rugby during the 1950s and gave the UAR the confidence to travel outside South America in 1965.

Argentina's willingness to tour resulted in their 1990 visit to the UK and Ireland which saw the Pumas suffer heavy defeats by England and Scotland. But the tour brought the Pumas back into the world game after the problems caused by the Falklands War. The Pumas may have been beaten heavily, but they gained valuable experience for their World Cup challenge.

Pablo Mamone is a Buenos Aires based rugby writer

The moment before Mendez, the Argentine prop, was sent off against England at Twickenham last year. His punch can be seen between Dooley (5) and Ackford (4). It was Ackford who was felled by the blow.

IT'S NOT THE WINNING THAT COUNTS (ALTHOUGH IT HELPS)

r many years now
atWest has
pported a wide
nge of sporting
ents from rugby to
tball to squash.
e're also active in
e Arts and
mmunity events.
e're proud to be
olved, and we
n to stay that way.

National Westminster Bank PLC, Registered Office 41 Lothbury, London EC2P 2BP.

AUSTRALIA: The Australian squad; they finished fourth in the 1987 World Cup.

AUSTRALIA

by
Greg Campbell

There have been few more memorable games of rugby than the 1987 World Cup semi-final between Australia and France. It was an exquisite, tantalising match which produced unforgettable tries, unforseen excitement and endless drama. France's epic 30–24 victory placed the inaugural World Cup series firmly on the international sporting map. And in the process, a mighty era of unprecedented success for Australian rugby began collapsing in dramatic fashion. After the record-breaking and historic victories during the 1984 Wallabies' Grand Slam campaign followed by a marvellous Bledisloe Cup winning series over the All Blacks in New Zealand, the 1987 World Cup was to be Australia's crowning glory. Instead it produced bitterness, controversy and, of course, failure.

It has been a stormy four years since for Australia. As is fast becoming the norm for Australian rugby, there has been as much drama off the field as on the playing paddock. Alan Jones, the voluble, demanding but successful coach, was sacked and replaced by Bob Dwyer – ironically the man whom Jones replaced four years earlier. And throughout his second term, Dwyer has had difficulty in keeping the restless natives content. Dwyer has managed to keep himself in the coaching job but the continual political fighting within the Australian Rugby Football Union council finally resulted in long-serving selectors John Bain and Bob Templeton both becoming casualties of the corridor warfare.

These battles are set to continue so long as personal egos and parochialism remain among officials. This scenario will continue to undermine World Cup campaigns until a united front is finally stitched together. It's not as though the players themselves don't have enough problems. Australian teams are forever

Australia's Tim Gavin brushes off a tackle from John Buckton, of England B, during the 1988 tour. Australia have consistently produced effective back row forwards at test level.

producing quality players who mature into world-class players only to see many lured away by a fistful of dollars and smart talking. It has been that way ever since Herbert Henry 'Dally' Messenger accepted a lucrative fee of £100 per match to switch codes and play rugby league in 1907.

Despite the daunting problems which erode the strength of the Wallabies, the foundations are, fortunately, secure. There may not be as many bricks (players) compared to many other rugby playing nations, but the foundation is well constructed and a proven success. There are only 26,500 senior players in Australia, but by the time they have graduated into the club ranks the quality players have been identified. Australia's small player base and even smaller major competition scene, which focuses chiefly on the Sydney and Brisbane club championships plus the growing Canberra premiership, is perhaps one of the Wallabies' greatest strengths. The national under-17 and under-21 championships combined with a highly successful schoolboys' programme and a developing scholarship system under the control of the Australian Institute of Sport see few outstanding players slip through the vast player-identification net. Since the introduction of the national coaching plan in the mid-1970s, Australia has risen from the position of the 'Woeful Wallabies' in 1972 and the embarrassing defeat by Tonga in 1973 to become a genuine world force in the 1980s and 1990s.

The domestic representative pinnacle leading to test selection has tradition-ally been the interstate series between New South Wales and Queensland. In recent years, the development of rugby in the Australian Capital Territory has seen both state teams engaged in a major fixture with the Canberra Kookaburras. The first of the NSW-Queensland matches was played in 1882 when the Northern Rugby Union, now the Queensland Rugby Union, was formed. Eight years earlier the Southern Rugby Union, now the NSW Rugby Union, was born. But rugby was of course played prior to the establishment of these bodies. History fails to clarify where and in what year rugby was first played in Australia, but Eldred Harmer told the NSW Parliament in 1864 that it had been played in Sydney for 'about 35 years' when he made his plea for the game to be outlawed.

It wasn't until 1899, however, that Australia played their first test. The match against Great Britain was played at the Sydney Cricket Ground and the Australians triumphed 13-3. This wasn't the first tour by an overseas nation, as England first toured in 1884. It was on this tour that the extent of Australian Football's popularity in the southern states was amplified. England were challenged to a game of Australian Football by Carlton after the tourists had thrashed Melbourne in rugby. Carlton understandably squared the ledger and strangely the Englishmen went on to play nineteen games of Australian Football and only sixteen games of rugby. Australian Football continues to have an irreversible stranglehold in the southern and western states, although rugby continues to grow in Western Australia where there has been a large influx of New Zealanders in recent years.

Coinciding with Australia's resurgence in the 1980s has been their increasing involvement with New Zealand teams. New Zealand has often been referred

to by NSW and Queensland teams as the University of Rugby. This continuous playing contact has led to the vast improvement of Australia's forward play, whilst the All Blacks have widened the armoury with a more lethal backline game. Trans-Tasman rugby contact resulted in the formation of the South Pacific Championship in 1987; but this tournament lapsed in 1991. The teams involved were NSW, Queensland, Auckland, Canterbury and Wellington plus Fiji.

While the successes of the Australian Schools teams since they first toured South Africa in 1969 have been magnificent, it has been the continual contact with New Zealand provincial teams and overseas touring teams which has enabled the bright young players gradually to step up in grade and class as they rise towards international selection. The long list of test players who have risen from Australian Schoolboy selection to win Wallaby honours reflects the value of the schools movement. Both the 1977–78 and 1981–82 Australian Schools teams which toured the United Kingdom undefeated contained ten future Wallabies. They also produced former Australian rugby league captain, Wally Lewis (1977–78) and Colin Scotts (1981–82) who was a third-round American Football draft choice and played with the Phoenix Cardinals and the Houston Oilers. Players such as Michael O'Connor (1977–78) and Ricky Stuart (1985) also became dual rugby union and rugby league internationals.

The continuing player drain, as a result of defections to rugby league, has seen a series of Wallaby coaches left frustrated by the loss of crucial players. In recent years, Dwyer has had to replace Matthew and Brad Burke, Brett Papworth, Andrew Leeds, James Grant, Steve Lidbury and Ricky Stuart. Fortunately the attacking nature of rugby league with its emphasis on ball handling and distribution has rubbed off onto Australian rugby players from an early age, which has resulted in Wallaby teams being blessed during the 1980s with gifted backs such as David Campese, Michael Lynagh, Nick Farr-Jones and Mark Ella. The rugby league defections, when added to the normal player retirements and tour unavailabilities, cause Australian rugby to turn over an unusually high quota of players resulting in a high number of new caps. This instability is largely responsible for Australia's inconsistent test

Ian Williams is one of world rugby's fastest wings. He gives Australia a real cutting edge on the right flank.

record – particularly during Dwyer's second term as coach. And if Australia is to rise from Pool Three and challenge for the Webb Ellis Trophy, then consistency during the World Cup is paramount.

Fortunately for the Australians, they have been blessed with a handful of truly world-class players who have formed the core of the team over the past six years. That erratic genius, David Campese, has no peer in world rugby when it comes to attacking artistry. His dazzling footwork, including his famous trademark, the 'goosestep', combined with his blistering acceleration, have scored the world record number of test tries. And, given that he is only 28 and still has many years of test rugby ahead, his eventual scoring tally seems destined to pass 50.

Fly-half Michael Lynagh is similarly placed. He holds the world record number of test points and is a year younger than Campese. Lynagh is not just a goal-kicking machine but a pivotal back who possesses playing vision and all-round skill. The third member of Australia's version of the 'Holy Trinity' is scrum-half Nick Farr-Jones. Farr-Jones is widely respected throughout the world – both on and off the field. He may not have the bullet-like pass of John Hipwell or the sparkle of Ken Catchpole but he has an unerring pass, the ability to spot an opening and the strength and vigour to link up with his forwards.

A number of new world-class players have emerged over the past two seasons. In August 1989, against the All Blacks, the national selectors opted for three untried youngsters in hooker Phil Kearns, loose head prop Tony Daly and centre Tim Horan. And months later, a second centre, Jason Little, blossomed on the Wallaby tour of France and Canada. Further quality was discovered in tight head prop Ewen McKenzie who continued to climb the learning curve. When he was eventually slotted alongside Kearns and Daly, Australia rediscovered a scrummaging power which had earlier entered rugby folklore when Andy McIntyre, Tom Lawton and Enrique Rodriguez spearheaded a famous Wallaby push-over try against Wales at Cardiff Arms Park in 1984. The new combination of Daly, Kearns and McKenzie were confirmed in their high international regard when they overshadowed the much-vaunted All Black scrum during last year's Wallaby Bledisloe Cup tour of New Zealand. The development of player depth on that tour plus the historic third test victory, which ended the All Blacks' 50 match winning-streak, put

The magical skills of David Campese are acknowledged throughout the rugby world. Despite being tackled by Steve Hackney (England B), he still gets the ball away.

Australia among the favourites for the 1991 World Cup. The Wallabies have demonstrated they will field a team strong in the basics of scrummaging and line-out play. This is balanced by some gifted individual backs plus a commitment to defence which kept the All Blacks tryless in the Wellington third test.

However, Australia are searching to plug holes in their arsenal; notably at fullback (if Campese is chosen on the wing), back-up support at fly-half and hooker plus finally settling on the best balanced backrow trio.

Steve Cutler towering above the Lions' pair of Dooley and Ackford in the second test of the 1989 series. His ball winning has been magnificent for Australia against the best line out men in the world.

The need to find and develop new young players and provide them with exposure to touring and European conditions led to the 1990 Emerging Wallabies tour of England, France, Italy, Spain and the Netherlands. It was a massive investment for the future by the ARFU and they hope a dividend will be quickly repaid.

Australia's semi-final loss to France, followed by a bitter last-minute loss to Wales in the play-off match, resulted in the Wallabies being seeded fourth for this World Cup. The final pool match with Wales represents the biggest hurdle prior to the quarter-finals. Both teams will have learned much about each other's strengths and weaknesses following Wales' short tour of Australia this summer. Over the past twelve years Australia and Argentina have engaged in a total of eight tests with Australia winning four, the Pumas three with one drawn. When the teams last met in 1987, Argentina became the first non-IRFB country to defeat Australia in a test series when winning the second test 27–19 after the first was drawn 19-all. This loss greatly contributed to the demise, months later, of coach Alan Jones.

Australia's contact with their other pool opponent, Western Samoa, has been mainly gained through the efforts of the Queensland Rugby Union. The QRU hosted a three-match tour of Queensland by Western Samoa in 1989 with the Reds downing the islanders 46–8 in the final match. Then last year Queensland travelled the Pacific and defeated Western Samoa 33–9. However, it must be said that Western Samoa were without their New Zealand and Australian playing contingent and the full advantage of these additional players was evident when they swept to World Cup qualifying success in Japan.

In 1991, Australia will be at longer odds to capture the World Cup than in 1987. There is no home town advantage, the cup is being played out of season and their playing record is not as formidable as it was prior to 1987. But it is a scenario which this Australian team will find both challenging and inspiring.

Greg Campbell is rugby correspondent for the *Australian*.

CANADA: *The Canadian squad;*
they emerged as champions of the America's qualifying group.

CANADA

by
Peter McMullan

Four years can be an age in the lifetime of a first class athlete and Canada is hoping the pause between the first and second World Cups will have refined and matured a squad that did better than probably anyone expected in New Zealand in 1987. True, Canada failed to progress beyond the first round, defeating Tonga 37–4 before losing to Ireland (46–19) and Wales (40–9). Heavy losses but far from routs as Ireland had to come from 19–16 behind in the last quarter while Wales were fortunate to be no more than 9–6 down at the interval.

Since 1987 Canada has expanded its horizons providing its top players with a fortified diet of first class opposition while, at the same time, bringing forward a new crop of talented younger players. Under-19 competition is strong across the country and is helping to identify potential internationals. Climatic conditions are such that while British Columbia plays a recognised northern hemisphere season, from September to May, the rest of the country turns to more traditional winter sports in late autumn and enjoys its rugby from April to October. The heart of the game is on the west coast and players from British Columbia will again be in a large majority when the World Cup squad is named.

Retirements have claimed lock Hans de Goede, an inspirational leader in 1987 in New Zealand, and his formidable partner to Ro Hindson. Together they won more than fifty caps dating back to the early seventies and, while de Goede was content to move on to coaching, Hindson, already Canada's most capped player came back at 38 for one more game. Argentina lost that match and Canada gained a 15–6 World Cup preliminary round win in March 1990. It was a remarkable effort by Canada's greatest ever forward and it also

Ron Toews, of Canada, loses the ball in the tackle during the popular Hong Kong Sevens tournament which provides welcome competition for the players.

provided a winning start for new coach Ian Birtwell, who had been preferred to his predecessor Gary Johnston when the position came up for regular review by the Canadian Rugby Union in the autumn of 1989. Ironically Johnston had just seen Canada achieve its biggest ever winning margin over the USA, 21–3 in Toronto. Birtwell's second game, against the USA in Seattle, in June was as forgettable as the Argentina win was memorable during 1990. The Eagles, with five new caps, were better motivated and earned a 14–12 success, albeit with a late penalty after Canada's captain, full-back and

Glen Ennis, the Canadian forward, bursts through a gap against Argentina leaving Hugo Porta behind. Ennis is a highly rated forward.

kicker Mark Wyatt, lost his usually confident touch. That left Canada with seven days to regroup for the decisive World Cup Americas Zone game with Argentina in Buenos Aires.

With established three-quarters Pat Palmer, a most effective wing, and Tom Woods, a force in the centre, unable to travel, Canada's backs included reserve scrum-half John Graf on the wing for his third cap and newcomer David Lougheed, a robust young full-back from Ontario, in the centre. On the day everything fell into place. Gareth Rees, playing in his tenth international after

Mark Wyatt, the experienced Canadian full-back whose place has been under threat in recent matches.

being overlooked for the USA match, was superb in all he did, supplying 15 points from a drop goal and four penalties in a 19–15 victory that stands high above all other Canadian results since their first two games played and lost in Japan in 1932.

That was long before rugby in Canada achieved its present status as a sport with upwards of 12,000 players in all ten provinces and an annual budget of more than $900,000 managed by the CRU's professional staff in Ottawa. Rugby comes under the umbrella of the federal government's Sport Canada ministry and benefits from annual funding of about $250,000 while commercial sponsors add another $100,000. With national programmes to run for both under-19 and under-21 groups, along with a very full senior campaign, money matters are given high priority at all times.

Come 1991 Canada will be ready for every eventuality and will have a team that, in terms of World Cup participation, could be the most experienced of them all. More than half of the first choice players from four years ago are still very much in contention and they have been reinforced by the arrival of men like Paul Szabo, a mobile prop who scored two tries for Rugby Canada, the national side in all but name, against Paul Thorburn's Wales 'B' in June 1989. That was the sensational game in Edmonton in which the home team came from 28–4 behind to lose 31–29. Then there is Al Charron, a rangy big Ontario forward in the New Zealand mould who turned in two outstanding displays against Argentina, and scrum-half Chris Tyan, a tough competitor in any company. Indeed, he and John Graf provide Canada with great depth in this critical position.

At full-back there is the absorbing competition between Scott Stewart (22) and Mark Wyatt (30). Wyatt, Canada's most capped international, first played in 1982 but was moved to the wing to allow Stewart his debut in 1989. Wyatt kicked five penalties and a conversion as the Canadians triumphed 21–3 in Toronto. Stewart remained as full-back for the British Columbia game with the 1989 All Blacks but Wyatt regained the No. 15 shirt in 1990 for the games with Argentina. It is a continuing headache for the selectors with Wyatt, who has kicked over 150 points for his country, vital to the side. Stewart, a fierce competitor, has youth and size on his side of the argument.

Competition is the key to success and there has been plenty of that as Canada has hosted Japan, Scotland and the USA in the run-up to the World Cup. Neither Canada nor the USA has managed a win against an International Board country. However, it would have been a different story from Victoria in 1989 but for the break-away try that allowed Ireland to snatch a hollow 24–21 victory in injury time at Centennial Stadium, setting for the athletic events in the 1994 Commonwealth Games. Fiji won more easily, 35–15 in Vancouver twenty-one years ago while Canada's previous encounters with France are a 24–9 defeat in Calgary in 1978, followed by a 34–15 loss to France 'A' in Paris the following year. There is a sense that the challenge of Fiji, Romania and France might just be within the compass of this seasoned and well balanced Canadian squad in this World Cup round of group matches.

Peter McMullan is a Canadian-based rugby writer.

ENGLAND:
The 1991 England Grand Slam winning squad.

ENGLAND

by
John Mason

England as befits the most zealous of converts, regard the World Cup not only as the pinnacle of competition but also the essential ingredient of rugby's welfare world-wide. From an attitude of downright hostility to the concept, the Rugby Football Union, the game's controlling authority in England, have embraced the cause passionately. Long gone are the days when RFU dignitaries wrinkled patrician noses in distaste at the thought of such a competition and blandly applied the block at those International Board meetings when either New Zealand or Australia dared to air the topic. The Bard knew what he was talking about when he claimed that in time the savage bull doth bear the yoke.

Within hours of miserable defeat by Wales in the 1987 quarter-finals – more about that abject encounter later – England's players and officials were promising that next time round there would be a vastly different story to tell. Mistakes in preparation would not be repeated and when the opportunity for lasting glory recurred, hopefully at Twickenham in 1991, the chance would be confidently and competently seized. The next World Cup campaign was beginning then and there on a damp, steamy day in down-town Brisbane.

Defeat hurt and the England contingent, captained by Mike Harrison, managed by Mike Weston and coached by Martin Green, did not attempt to conceal their feelings. No one pretended that England might have lowered the colours of the All Blacks in the semi-finals but they insisted vigorously that they would have taken third place, subsequently occupied by Wales who beat Australia in the play-off for the minor positions, in the inaugural competition.

Less than three years previously the RFU, in their wisdom, were of the view that such a tournament would be divisive, besides pandering to erratic Antipodean whims. It would also be bowing to the incipient spread of commercialism and treading an unacceptable path towards the forbidden fruits of professionalism. In short, a World Cup was unnecessary. That, I ought to explain, was the majority view of English officialdom. Players and coaches thought differently and here and there committee room voices were raised in their support. Rugby, regrettably, rarely listens to those who pay at the gate but, and I think the generalisation is permissible, among the rank and file there was a widespread belief that the sooner England stepped aboard that particular gravy train the better. The average punter, after all, cheerfully exercises the rights of judge and jury, either mourning or delighting in England's gloriously inconsistent passage in international competition. The roller-coaster that is English rugby possesses more highs and lows than those that regularly reduce the Met. Office computers to impotence.

Happily, there was the odd visionary who had penetrated the RFU's tightly-bound ranks and despite the earnest exhortations of those who feared the consequences of such a competition, that minority in favour were permitted to state a case. It has been fashionable for years to hammer the RFU with any stick that comes to hand. Much of the criticism has been as unfounded as it has been unfair. Those minority voices were heard and, though it took time, the due processes of democracy and debate led to a change of heart.

None was more important in that passage of history than the late John MacGregor Kendall Kendall-Carpenter, whose tall, lean, sinewy figure loped along the corridors of rugby power, nationally and internationally, for forty years as player and administrator. His death in May 1990 was not only an occasion for the English to mourn. In many ways if there was one person who had ensured by his actions that a Rugby Union World Cup would become the single most important event in the history of the game, that individual was John Kendall-Carpenter, past captain of Truro School, Oxford University, Penzance-Newlyn, Bath, Cornwall, Barbarians and England.

Against formidable odds and, ultimately, I suggest, at the cost of his health, Kendall-Carpenter, a former president of the International Rugby Board, the Rugby Football Union and, at the time of his death, president of the English Schools' Union, has provided a lasting legacy. His powers of persuasion convinced the doubters, mostly in the northern hemisphere, that the idea of a world competition was not only workable but also a necessary step in the development of rugby football world-wide. The elegance of his language, the

The Blackpool Tower; Wade Dooley, the England lock, is backed up by Mike Teague in the special match to mark the centenary of the Barbarians club.

dryness of his schoolmaster wit, the utter determination to carry the project through and an in-born restlessness were his weapons – plus a well-thumbed passport and a body-clock so adaptable that the world's time zones existed for lesser mortals. He was chairman of the first as well as the second organising committee, and in the weeks immediately before he died was preparing to retire early from the headship of Wellington School, Somerset, so as to devote himself full-time to the 1991 World Cup responsibilities.

This giant among men could spectacularly mis-judge the timing or content

Mike Teague, the British Lions Player of the Series in Australia in 1989. Teague is a world class blind-side forward who can also play No 8.

of a public speech. He could zoom off at inconsequential tangents as the mood took him and he was a master of the acid rebuke so splendidly well-turned that he appeared to be awarding compliments. He was also a person to whom rugby football world-wide owes a debt that cannot be repaid. Ostensibly he was English, the epitome of suave, erudite excellence. As it happens he was born in Wales, though that in this context is irrelevant. He was a citizen of the world – and Cornwall, his true home – and without him not only would England not be involved in the 1991 World Cup, the event itself would not exist.

In 1987 England had an easy run to the quarter-finals as, in addition to Australia, their Pool One opponents were Japan and the United States. Their 60 points against the Japanese stand as an English record and though losing to Australia in the opening match at the ill-fated Concord Oval in Sydney, England had their hosts on the run for long periods. David Campese was permitted the most fortuitous of tries in that he, too, thought he had not scored. The referee said that he had and stiff English upper lips trembled only fractionally. Not only is the referee's word final, he is infallible. The laws sustain that belief which is a cornerstone of the game and it matters not a tinker's cuss, foul play apart, what a video tape may show to the contrary.

That was England's introduction to World Cup rugby and having competently disposed of the challenge of the US Eagles and the Japanese, the next stop on the road was at a well-appointed housing estate not too far from Brisbane's city hospital where some Welshmen lay in wait at Ballymore. The match that England and Wales presented as a rugby World Cup quarter-final was so dreadful that even the winners were embarrassed: well certainly until the scars of the subsequent mauling by New Zealand in the semi-finals had healed.

For the record Wales won 16–3 on 8 June, 1987, in the first match between the countries to be played in the southern hemisphere. Only one of the three Welsh tries had anything about it at all, such was the English carelessness and inefficiency. Paul Thorburn, restored as the Wales captain in October 1990, converted two of the tries and England, so engulfed by stage-fright that they froze, countered with a penalty goal. The succinct summing-up by Frank O'Callaghan, the then rugby correspondent of Brisbane's *Courier Mail*, and an old friend, still raises a wry smile: 'If I say I enjoyed it, do you promise not to bring those teams back here again . . .' he insists that his subsequent retirement has had nothing to do with that miserable afternoon.

The inquests began early, not least in the Welsh camp. They, too, had not been fooled by victory. By the rules of the competition, having been beaten, England had to return home as soon as was reasonably possible. The airline schedules were such that they had gone before lunch the following day. Greatly to his credit, Mike Weston, England's manager, found the time to call a press conference in his hotel room after breakfast on 9 June. Happy occasion it was not, honest it was.

At this stage of the proceedings some four years later, the general drift of Weston's comments is more important than the precise detail. Continuity, development programmes, a secure representative ladder, early identification of the better players, a viable league competition and constructive coaching were some of the things touched upon. Pleas to establish a national pattern of play were given an airing and, above all, tribute was paid to the simplicity of the All Blacks' game and its attendant virtues of speed, support and commonsense: the uncomplicated efficient practice of basic skills.

While Weston's masterly summary of the 1987 event, as well as his carefully considered thoughts about the best way forward for England in the future, did not gain the universal approval it deserved, he did succeed in disturbing complacency in high places.

Annoyed at the way in which Martin Green, the coach, had been treated, and though re-appointed himself, Weston found it necessary to resign. So drastic a solution left no room for manoeuvre but, if nothing else, it at least silenced the more vocal critics as well as ensuring his successor, Geoff Cooke, a clear field.

Brian Moore, the England and British Lions hooker, has said in another context that all members of the Rugby Football Union should be automatically retired at 55. While the observation should not be taken too literally, Moore was echoing a remark by an equally successful England player of another era. Bob Hiller, whose goal-kicking used to win matches in the days when

Mine! The betting would be on Dean Richards, the England No 8 (centre) reaching the ball. He has battled back from a serious shoulder injury to prove he is vital to England's cause.

England were incapable of scoring tries, believed that once a player had been out of the first-class game for three years he was struggling to keep up with current developments, the problems and, most important of all, the solutions. Not even Moore, scourge of the inefficient, scornful of the superficial, has gone that far.

Though I will refrain – well, perhaps, not – from trotting out the hoary contention about statistics, statistics and damned lies, last year even the most redoubtable of opponents began casting glances, some tentative, some admiring, some mocking but none unaware, at England's progress. No matter the tendency to freeze on the big occasion – Brisbane v Wales 1987, Murrayfield v Scotland 1990 – when a side can score 166 points, including 25 tries, in a run of four matches against World Cup opposition, a definitive case

has been stated. Fiji, Ireland, Wales and Argentina would vouch for it. France, too, the beaten finalists in 1987, would not be above the odd complimentary word after the way they were mauled by England at Twickenham in 1989 and again in 1990 in Paris.

Jamie Salmon, unique in recent times as an Englishman who has played for New Zealand (not the other way about, to correct wrong impressions in high places) is convinced that the England side of the last two seasons or so is at least as good as the Grand Slam team of 1980 led by Bill Beaumont. 'Comparisons may be odious,' says Salmon, 'but I believe that the spine of the 90 side – hooker, locks, No. 8, scrum-half, outside-half and fullback – match their predecessors. As a back I could be drummed out of the club but I accept that without our friends the donkeys up front, we would not get a sniff of the carrot, let alone the ball.'

This is an age in which a team manager can say without contradiction, in what still passes as an amateur game, that he has a group of players in, and on the fringes of the squad, 'who – I quote – recognise the requirements for success at international level and who are prepared to modify their total lifestyles and commit them fully in pursuit of that aim.' The words are those of Geoff Cooke, England's manager, whose mild, courteous manner can be, in the nicest sense, misleading. Beneath it beats a heart dedicated to making England successful and for those that have not pulled their weight, the sharp words from the manager have been salutary. High on his list of criticisms, not that his public stance seeks controversy, is that players have been reluctant, or unable, to embrace fully what he describes a 'total rugby' concept which, in turn, mirrors what has been happening in England's clubs every Saturday.

'Far too much of our (English) rugby', says Cooke, 'is based on a safety first approach with an obsession for the set pieces and kicking as the main tactical planks. Few clubs appear to be working on the development of individual players and equally few producing any back play of note.

'Although the league programme has sharpened the competitive edge of our

OPPOSITE: Richard Hill, the combative England scrum-half. Hill has captained his country.

OVERLEAF: The rugby jersey is hard to recognise but the player is easy. Jeremy Guscott, the England centre, pictured helping the Four Home Unions beat Europe.

players and is developing greater mental toughness under pressure, we must be aware of the potential dangers of the fear of failure, which still seems to be an inhibiting factor at international level.'

These judgements, calmly delivered and carefully discussed before and after, could be said to have had an effect. Those 166 points and 25 tries in four matches at Twickenham against Fiji, Ireland, Wales and Argentina, all 1991 World Cup finalists, are irrefutable evidence, though the figures only hint at the style. As in the same period France were overwhelmed at the Parc des Princes, England, it might be deduced, have not been lacking for motivation – a far cry from that dreary June afternoon in Brisbane in 1987.

Cooke's management team of Roger Uttley, coach, and John Elliott, selector, has been in place sufficiently long that even talk of England's arrangements and preparations for the 1995 World Cup does not grate. Better, of course, the manager grants with a ghost of a smile, that they go into that tournament as defending champions. Such forward planning is a legitimate exercise in the building of a team, plus the mostly unsung back-up contingent, and in those respects there has been a briskly matter-of-fact approach by

England ever since Mike Weston, Cooke's predecessor, assessed the damage done by the quarter-final defeat and set about attempting to ensure that there would be no repetition.

A tiny illustration from the France-New Zealand match in Paris in November 1990 encapsulates what Cooke, who was present, has been saying about the exercise of skills and the ability to turn training drills into practice when required – the expertise, in effect, that wins World Cups. That little touch of class came when Gary Whetton, New Zealand's captain and lock, waved his hands even as Grant Fox was shaping to kick-off. The urgent hand signal from Whetton meant 'keep it short'. Fox obliged to the centimetre. New Zealand

OPPOSITE: *Will Carling, England's Grand Slam captain, shows why he is so difficult to pin down.*

BELOW: *Flanker Peter Winterbottom moves the ball to England team mate Rory Underwood as he is tackled.*

got the scrum, France erred – three more points for the All Blacks as Fox drilled the ball high between the posts.

The Fox points, and there have been more than 400 in internationals alone, are the oil that permits the other parts of the machine to continue operating smoothly should the opposition, as has been England's besetting ambition for the past four years, find that accommodating, multi-purpose spanner to toss into the works. There is genuine admiration, too, for the New Zealand formula, though the approach, and the playing styles, are different. England, whose competitive structure of 1,138 clubs in 114 leagues, incorporating promotion and relegation nation-wide, is the biggest in the world, know what they must do to achieve that metaphorical crock of gold at the end of the Twickenham rainbow. To succeed, each cog in the machine has a job, a ratchet clicking inexorably into position to exert the maximum pressure with the minimum of effort. The process must be repeated without let or hindrance for six times eighty minutes: eight hours of rugged commitment, of power and pace and perception – a happy mix, too, of inspiration and perspiration and, above all, efficiency. If the White Tornadoes, to dub England with the mildly mocking but not unaffectionate nickname we media camp followers have awarded them, manage that, their World Cup challenge will have genuine substance. To bracket England with New Zealand is a proposition which even as recently as 1988, following the two test defeats in Australia, would have been preposterous. But as long as the principal cutting edge of the England squad continues to be precisely honed that is no longer the case.

England are second favourites for the Cup and their magnificent Grand Slam achievement this year has proved to the players that they can be winners at the highest level. Simon Hodgkinson kicked a record 60 points in the championship, and the players were carried from the Twickenham pitch after clinching the Grand Slam with victory over France. The disappointment of previous seasons was replaced by unconcealed joy.

Alex Wyllie, the All Blacks coach, conceded last autumn in France that unless the world champions were firing on all cylinders – with true New Zealander economy of words what he actually said was 'if we don't give it a go!' – the challenge of Scotland and England would be hard to contain. That is the nearest to a concession Wyllie, or his countrymen, are likely to make –and that was off the field. It will be noted that there was no reference to

France, though at that point there was a test series to complete. Not even the Frenchmen present demurred.

New Zealand's next appearance in the northern hemisphere will be at Twickenham on Thursday, 3 October, 1991, at 2.30 pm. Be there.

John Mason is rugby correspondent for the *Daily Telegraph*.

Rob Andrew enjoys the Grand Slam moment! The England outside-half is carried off the Twickenham pitch after this year's win over France.

FIJI: *The Fijian squad;*
they qualified by right for this year's World Cup.

FIJI

FIJI R.U.

by
Greg Campbell

There has long been a fervour about rugby which has echoed through the valleys of Wales and across the border regions of Scotland. But in tiny Fiji, the very mention of the word rugby whips the local islanders into a frenzy. For a country with no television and where hero worshipping can only be done via newspapers and radio, the popularity of the game is remarkable and growing significantly in stature each year. Make no mistake, the importance of the World Cup has no limits in Fiji.

Ever since Fiji embarked on their first overseas tour – an ambitious eight-match tour of New Zealand in 1939 – the rugby world has had little idea of what to expect. By the end of that tour, Fiji rugby stamped itself indelibly on the international rugby map when winning seven games and drawing one –the only international team ever to tour New Zealand unbeaten. But what the statistics didn't reveal was the Fijian playing style. It is a style which is positively unorthodox but thoroughly exciting and entertaining, as the world rugby public has since witnessed.

As far as the Fijians are concerned, flair is definitely not an SOS distress signal. Many of their ambitious passing movements derive from being caught under intense pressure deep within their own territory. Their playing style reflects a carefree manner; the very thought of ruck, maul and scrum is too much like hard work. This is one of the reasons why Fiji has excelled at sevens rugby – notably the Cathay Pacific Hongkong Bank Championship.

Fiji's delightful, running game dates back to 1884 when matches were first played between Fijians of the local constabulary and travelling British soldiers. Now, 107 years later, Fiji boasts over 20,000 players despite lack of funding, equipment and coaching schemes. For decades, Fiji has relied heavily on the generosity, both in cash and in kind, of the New Zealand and Australian Rugby Football Unions. During the 1980s Fiji established concrete playing links with both New Zealand and Australia through the South Pacific Championship, in which the national team opposed the provincial heavy-weights of Auckland, Canterbury, Wellington, Queensland and New South Wales. Fiji may not have been a championship contender, but they have scored several surprise victories and have always proved difficult to beat in the heat and energy-sapping humidity of Suva's Government Stadium where they are strongly supported by a fanatical crowd.

Fiji's unpredictability extends to their results. One day they can be potential world beaters and rank minnows the next. During the last World Cup, Fiji comfortably defeated Argentina 28–9 but were flogged 74–13 by the All

BELOW: *Severo Koroduadua is surrounded by Frenchmen during Fiji's 31–16 defeat in the 1987 World Cup quarter finals.*

OPPOSITE: *The Fijian defence fails to stop Tony Stranger, of Scotland, scoring at Murrayfield. Fiji are happier on the attack.*

Blacks and were surprisingly beaten 18–15 by Italy. They reached the quarter-finals on percentages and gave France, the eventual cup runners-up, a mighty fright before they were elbowed aside 31–16. Few people will ever forget the skilful Severo Koroduadua losing the ball without a defender in sight and the try line begging to be crossed. That incident seemed to typify Fijian rugby.

Fiji has achieved tremendous results over the years, with their 25–21 win over the 1977 British Lions ranking amongst the best. It has long been considered that Fiji would be a true world force if discipline could be instilled into their game and if their forwards could become truly competitive in the set pieces. A plentiful supply of possession blended with their pace and adventure would make Fiji one of the most difficult teams to defeat. An example of their all-round pace came when Fiji were dismantling New South Wales in 1983. As a Fijian player sprinted through the New South Wales defences, Peter Lucas, the former Wallaby No. 8, gave chase and eventually dragged down his opponent only metres from the line. Lucas later revealed the only reason he

The try that set the Hong Kong Sevens final alight in 1990. Tomasi Cama Neisenirosi leaves John Gallagher of New Zealand behind.

gave a sustained chase was because the player had No. 3 on his back!

In an attempt to generate discipline into their game, former New Zealand provincial coach George Simpkin was invited to be Fiji's coaching director in the mid 1980s. Although he later moved to Hong Kong, Simpkin's influence has surfaced as their set play has become more stable and profitable. Simpkin, along with former Wallaby coach Alan Jones – a friend of the Fiji Rugby Union president and Prime Minister Ratu Sir Kaimasese Mara – are used as technical consultants despite residing outside Fiji. Along with their improved game, the Fijians have demonstrated growing self-discipline with regard to foul play, although England players may argue differently with three islanders sent off in the 1988 and 1989 clashes.

Another reason for Fiji's inconsistency has been their high player turnover.

Continual change of coaches lead to playing changes, with the selectors finding it difficult to retain faith in players. The poor economic condition of the country has seen many players leave for Australia and New Zealand where they can not only continue to play rugby but also support their families with better sources of income. The most notable Fijian loss was former test fly-half Acura Niuqila who moved to Australia and toured England, Scotland and Italy with the 1988 Wallabies.

There has long been argument within the Pacific islands over why Fiji was given automatic World Cup status in 1987 ahead of its neighbours Tonga and Western Samoa. The three countries compete in an annual Triangular series with Western Samoa now emerging as a real Pacific force. Unlike Western Samoa, whose team has been fortified by players from New Zealand, Fiji has chiefly relied on the locals from Rewa, Nadi, Lautoka and Suva. Suva has proved to be the dominant team over the past two years, and they have retained the Fairweather Sullivan Trophy – Fiji's version of New Zealand's Ranfurly Shield.

During this year's World Cup, Fiji will be based in France where they will oppose France, Canada (winners of the Americas' zone) and Romania (runners-up of the European zone). Although Canada and Romania are two of the world's most improved rugby nations, Fiji must again be hopeful of a quarter-final berth.

Fiji have 'warmed up' for the cup with a series of matches against New Zealand and Australian provincial teams plus Tests this summer against England and Tonga. In order to prepare their players for the cold European climate – which many of them have never experienced – Fiji finalised their cup preparation with a short tour of New Zealand's south island, including a fixture with the powerful Otago province before moving north to play the strong Waikato outfit.

Fiji has undoubtedly come a long way since their players took to the field without boots (they regarded them as uncomfortable impediments!). Although efforts have been made to improve their forward play, they are still second-class compared to the likes of France and will suffer accordingly. However, give them an inch and they'll take the proverbial mile.

Greg Campbell is rugby correspondent for the *Australian*.

FRANCE: *The French squad.*
Runners up in the 1987 World Cup.

FRANCE

by
John Reason

France should have won the Five Nations championship, or Grand Slam, every year during the 1980s. The Four Home Unions had sunk to such depths that with players like Serge Blanco, Phillipe Sella, Laurent Rodriguez and Jean-Pierre Rives they should have won every match. They did not do so and neither did they play well in the final of the 1987 World Cup against New Zealand. What was worse they collapsed. By the end of the decade, France's game was so confused and so totally lacking in direction that their clubs were combing the rest of the world for playing imports rather than develop their abundant native talent.

That was a tragedy not only for French rugby but for European rugby as well because Europe badly needed a worthy champion. Beyond that, it was a calamity for the game worldwide. Since the last war, France have introduced more flair and innovation and more technical advances in the actual playing of the game than any other country in the world. Arguably, they have been more innovative than the rest of the world put together. In the last ten years, that fountain of ideas has dried up. Instead of a bubbling and exciting stream, we have been left with an arid gully. We have all been the poorer for it and can only hope the optimists in French rugby are right when they say there are still enough good players to mount a worthwhile challenge for the 1991 World Cup.

All they need is to find and assemble the right players and point them in the right direction. Judging by the wreckage lying on the floor after a shaky New Zealand team had demolished two entirely different teams representing France within the space of eight days last year (90), that may not be an easy operation. Add to this, the off the field problems revolving around Albert Ferrasse, the

Getting downward pressure. Jean-Baptiste Lafond about to score one of his two tries against Wales in Cardiff in 1986. He is still an important part of the French set up.

President of the French Rugby Federation, and you have a rugby nation in turmoil.

The French, like the Italians and like the British and Irish, have played a form of handling football for hundreds of years, but the version of it that was codified at Rugby School was not introduced into France until the second half of the nineteenth century.

Then, in 1872, a rugby club was formed in Le Havre. Obviously, the game had been played there for some time before that, just as it had been played at Cambridge University, but the fact is that the first official rugby club in France was formed in Le Havre in the same year as the first official rugby club was formed at Cambridge University.

It was perhaps inevitable that the game's jump across the English Channel should land first at a port, where the phlegmatic locals gazed with some curiosity at a game which was so clearly a development of their own traditional game of *soule* . French dictionaries in England do not exactly bristle

Laurent Rodriguez, of France, about to be halted by Craig Chalmers, the Scotland outside-half, at Murrayfield in 1990. Rodriguez helped his country into the 1987 World Cup final.

with the word *soule*, but those British and Irish players who have played club rugby in France will immediately associate the word with *soulier*, which is the French word for slipper. And slipper, of course, is the euphemism by which British players refer to the way the boot goes in to any player foolish enough to go down on the ball in France. I can hear the snorts about that coming from New Zealand even now. They reckon they invented that particular use of the word slipper.

Be that as it may, and whatever the connection, it was equally inevitable that rugby would not set the place alight if it stayed in Le Havre. Fishermen are not that kind of people. In any case, they spend more of their waking hours on water than on land. However, as soon as the game spread south of the line in France where the vine starts growing, rugby flourished and became as fruitful as the grape itself. Real interest in this English version of *soule* first developed along the banks of the river Gironde leading to Bordeaux. It was an ecstatic partnership, perhaps the most felicitous landing that rugby has ever made.

Philippe Sella has the ball and considerable support as England's Jeremy Guscott makes the tackle. Sella is one of world rugby's most dynamic centres.

English companies, some of them based in or near Bristol, followed the British soldiers of fortune remaining from the Napoleonic Wars and did much to develop the French wine trade. So they were able to combine pleasure with pleasure by making some of the world's greatest wines, making money, making friends, and introducing all three as essential adjuncts to playing rugby. The French loved it.

As a result, the game became more firmly established in the poorer areas south of the river Loire. Life there was much harder than in the rich industrial plains of the North. It still is. But the people of the South have a warmer and a more relaxed temperament and a love of the romantic. The new game combined something of the old football with some of the movements and much of the bravado of the matador. It had a powerful appeal which it has retained. As a social phenomenon, though, it was exactly the reverse of what happened in England. There, the game was developed by young men who had been fortunate enough to go to public schools and universities. In France, it was the humble people working in agriculture in the South who took the game to their hearts. In essence, it was the same kind of development as took place in New Zealand, Australia and South Africa. There was one significant difference. The French are a practical people. They see no harm at all in paying those who are good enough at any activity to be clearly recognised as public entertainers. It soon became apparent that some of those French farmers had become delightful rugby players – so good, in fact, that it really was a terrible waste to leave them playing in front of two men and a dog in their local village. So they were persuaded to move by a little financial inducement.

Inevitably inter-club rivalries soon developed. Long before the First World War, the passions aroused by rugby in France led to unruly crowds. As early as 1913, only seven years after France had played international rugby for the first time against England, the International Board wrote to France to protest about the threatening behaviour of the crowd to both the referee and the Scottish players after France had played Scotland in Paris. The Board warned, what was then the governing body in France, that international matches with France would have to cease unless adequate steps were taken to prevent a recurrence of such trouble. The French then launched what has since developed into a national characteristic of promising to be good boys without ever really doing very much about it. The English, the Irish and the Welsh were mollified. The Scots were not. They refused to play France in 1914.

The appalling casualties of the Great War healed the breach, but France were not in the least abashed by what had happened in 1913. Indeed, they applied to join the International Board themselves, and repeated their application in 1920. In those days, England had the controlling votes on the Board, and refused the applications. If the sport was to remain amateur, it was as well that England did maintain a position of some reserve, because rugby spread so rapidly

OVERLEAF: *Franck Mesnel is held by both Will Carling and Jeremy Guscott with Rob Andrew making it a hat-trick of tacklers. Mesnel has formed a superb partnership with Sella in the French mid-field.*

He would not win many beauty contests but Pascal Ondarts is a massive figure in the front row war. He can play in any of the three front row positions.

through France and was received so enthusiastically that French rugby soon found itself facing exactly the same dilemma which had faced English rugby when the Northern clubs broke away to form the Rugby League thirty years earlier. The causes of the difficulties were the same, too. The popular appeal of rugby was such that clubs were able to take large sums of money at the gate, and a fair proportion of that money soon found its way into the pockets of the players, particularly the good ones.

The Four Home Unions could not have been all that well informed about the exact mechanics of the professionalism, because the heartlands of French rugby were far more remote than they are today, but the French were so carelessly imprudent the detective job was elementary. French players also thought nothing of switching from Rugby Union to Rugby League and back again. The catalyst for all this player bargaining was the French club championship. The French could see no point at all in playing unless there was a bit of competition involved. The Four Home Unions kept bleating about the game being concerned with friendly matches between clubs, but as far as the French were concerned, friendly matches only served to get the players fit for the real thing. Us versus Them. In a championship. For a Cup.

Accordingly, the French inaugurated a club championship in 1906, only twenty-three years after the first recorded game between two French clubs. As a consequence, the French club championship is the oldest national club championship in the world.

In those days, French international rugby was patronisingly dimissed as second class, so it must have come as a nasty shock to the Scots when France beat them in 1911. This was France's first victory in international rugby, and although it took France another forty years to really get their wagon rolling, they caught up so rapidly after the Second World War that by 1978 they had achieved parity with Scotland in the international series between the two countries and had overhauled Ireland.

The years between had been painful for France. In the 1920's, the Four Home Unions had watched with increasing distaste as France went on blithely with their club championship. At the end of the 1930–31 season, the Four Home Unions decided they had had enough, and broke off all playing contact with France. They added that they would not resume fixtures until the French Rugby Federation, which had replaced the first French governing body, had done what was necessary to ensure Rugby Union football in France was an amateur game. That was never really done, but the Second World War created an alliance which went beyond rugby and persuaded the British and Irish Unions to try again. Fixtures with France were resumed in 1947, but for years after that the International Board members were still worrying about the amateur *bona fides* of French Rugby. Those concerns were justified.

It seems strange, now that England, Scotland, Ireland and Wales all have club championships, to recall that international rugby relations between those countries and France were permanently under threat because the French refused to give up their own club championship. This was the central concern and as late as 1952 the French Federation felt their international fixtures were under such a threat that they agreed to abolish the club championship. They announced that this was the unanimous decision of the Federation's committee. This saved France from another visit to the international guillotine. Again, though, the promise to be good boys was never actually carried into practice, because the outraged French clubs simply would not let it happen. They kept their championship!

The Four Home Unions were still tut-tutting away in 1957, and asking for assurances and all the rest of it. The French, under the astute M. Renee Crabos were still tut-tutting away in unison and saying how very difficult it all was, and why not have another glass of this cheeky little 1947 Chateau Latour? The poor bloody infantry in the playing communities of Britain and Ireland had long ago decided that rugby in France was something special, and that going there was even better. For one thing, food in France was not rationed, as it had been in the UK for years after the war, and for another, the wine cost practically nothing.

Their generals soon got the message. By 1958, the International Board had, to all intents and purposes, given up the struggle to reform the French. From that moment, the attitude towards semi-professionalism in rugby football began to slide towards the position occupied with such enthusiasm by France, rather than the other way round. All France did was go on doing what they always had done. Ever so gradually, most of the Four Home Unions found themselves doing much the same until, in the autumn of 1990, the International Board voted to relax the laws relating to amateurism to the point where M. Albert Ferrasse was able to raise his eyebrows and tut-tut that he had intended to vote against such extravagant concessions to professionalism, but if that was what the rest of the world wanted . . . He did keep a straight face, bless him.

The re-admission of France to international rugby after the war had a profound influence on the game throughout the world. At first, it was simply a manifestation of style and ambition. A succession of brilliant backs who had grown up with the confidence of invariably playing running rugby with a dry ball on a dry pitch, took that confidence and those skills into the national team and showed them round the world.

However, it went even further than that. France swept aside the convention that forwards were only workhorses whose job it was merely to win the ball and then trot along behind while the prima donnas in the backs had all the fun.

Pierre Berbizier launches another French raid from a ruck. The scrum-half has lived through the Fouroux period in charge of the team.

The French forwards removed the old demarcation lines and wrote their own job specifications. As they got the ball first, forwards like Jean Prat, Benoit Dauga and Walter Spanghero handled the thing with such enthusiasm and such dexterity and such power that even the Springboks and the New Zealand All Blacks sat up and took notice, especially after France won a Test series in South Africa. The giants of the southern hemisphere even did a little discreet copying!

For a time, French forwards could not compete physically with the forwards of the world's first division rugby countries, but twenty years after infant welfare was introduced in France, a French rugby forward grew tall enough to break through the 6 ft 2 in barrier for the first time. By 1976, Andy Leslie, the captain of the All Blacks, was smiling ruefully about the fact that every so-and-so club in France had at least two forwards who were bigger than the All Blacks. By 1977, France had a pack of mastodons with Bastiat, Palmie and Imbernon. They did not eat grass, either. They ate meat. Red meat. In

Olivier Roumat, as he shows here, has given France a new dimension to their play – a real line out jumper. He will play a major role in the French bid for this World Cup.

addition, they had genuinely world class props of the calibre of Paparemborde and Cholley and they had two flankers as supreme as Rives and Skrela. They had the Spangheros, too, and a host of others, but they just could not squeeze them all into their team.

The 1977 side won the Grand Slam for France but it did it by playing a style of rugby which was inimical to France's spectacular traditions. Those massive tight-forwards did not concern themselves with fripperies. They crushed. Nor was that all. The little man sitting in the armchair at scrum-half behind them delighted so much in what they did and the way that they did it, that he resolved if ever he got into a position to influence the way France played the game, that was what France would do. The name of that scrum-half was Jacques Fouroux. Albert Ferrasse, the President of the French Rugby Federation, not only put him in charge of the French team for ten years, but clearly also saw in him someone whom he could adopt as Crown Prince in the hierarchy of the Federation.

Both these developments caused great controversy in France. Both had contentious outcomes, and the second resolved itself in a way that Albert Ferrasse could hardly have envisaged when, in 1990, Jacques Fouroux challenged the man who had been his patron for the presidency of the Federation. The gloves came off with a vengeance.

By then, sadly, French Rugby had forsaken its heritage and had collapsed into its most parlous state for fifty years. The articulate and intelligent club coaches in the country, men like Pierre Villepreux and Daniel Herrero, had no doubt that the man responsible for that demise was Jacques Fouroux. He had pursued his dream and had not only seen it shattered, but had shattered French rugby's faith in itself. For six or seven of those years, France still had a depth of playing resources unrivalled in Europe, and they had as much success in the Five Nations championship as anyone else. They even reached the final of the 1987 World Cup in New Zealand. But that was not the point.

John Reason is rugby correspondent for the *Sunday Telegraph*.

IRELAND: The Ireland squad;
they qualified by right for the World Cup finals.

IRELAND

by
David Walsh

There was a time when those who carried the torch for Irish rugby could take a breather and reflect on life's lighter side. Moss Keane, that colonel in the Dad's Army side of the early 1980s, once told the troops they were part of the worst Irish team to have won the wooden spoon! The lads would have understood big Moss.

You see, that was a decade ago, a different era in international rugby. Those were the days when Ireland could go into the pawn shop on Lansdowne Road and trade their wooden spoon for a Triple Crown. Self-deprecation came easily because the next big win was never more than a match away. The Irish would lose two or three matches, be excluded from all serious evaluations, ridicule themselves, take offence when others ridiculed them and then produce the big performance at Lansdowne Road. There, on a day rife with inspired insubordination, they would hit anything that moved and if it didn't move, they still hit it.

Keane played in the 1982 side that won the Triple Crown. The preparation for that achievement had been a seven match losing sequence. Another losing run began in 1984, stretched to five consecutive losses and ended in the Triple Crown of the following season. It was easy to laugh then. Ireland were the kind of team that nobody dared to dismiss. Since that Triple Crown of 1985, Ireland has played twenty matches in the Five Nations Championship (excluding 1991) and won just five. Two defeats out of four matches used to be an acceptable rate of failure, now it is three out of four and nobody is sure that the downturn is part of the old cycle. Quite the contrary, pessimism is the prevailing mood. We sit in the stand, fearing the worst. Light at the end of the tunnel? First, the tunnel has to be located.

Two factors have combined to dim the Irish star. The traditional shortage of quality players has become an acute problem and two positions represent, in microcosm, the greater struggle. Phil Orr, the loose-head prop, played twelve seasons of international rugby before retiring after the 1987 World Cup. Orr's passing left a wound in the Irish front row, one from which the team has yet to recover. Where do you go without an adequate loose head prop?

The search to unearth a quality openside flanker has been equally thorough but no more rewarding. Fergus Slattery had 61 caps when he retired after fifteen seasons in 1984. Out of the blue, Nigel Carr came along. Not a Slattery but a decent follow-up before a terrorist bomb ended Carr's career and left Ireland pursuing a successor who did not exist. Ireland's natural penchant for disruption depends upon the open flanker being quick, brave and fiercely competitive.

Running alongside Ireland's traditional difficulty is the progress achieved by France, England and Scotland. The French were the first to build a genuine organisation and how Ireland suffered. Ireland has not won in Paris since Ray McLoughlin carried the ball and a couple of Pyrenean-types across the line at the Stade Colombes in 1972. McLoughlin went on to become a millionaire businessman and on future visits to Paris Ireland went to pieces. A wing called Freddie McLennan scored an Irish try in the French capital ten years ago and there hasn't been one since. And that isn't the complete story. Fergus Slattery mis-timed a pass to Robbie McGrath in the Grand Slam match of 1982 and, through the 1980s, that would be recalled as Ireland's only try scoring chance at the Parc des Princes. The more perceptive amongst Ireland's following saw the dark days which lay ahead. Thankfully, it took England much longer to come to their senses. The turning point came at the World Cup in 1987 when England realised they could either compete with the thoroughbreds or the donkeys. Geoff Cooke and a few older heads in the side have steered them into the top league and far away from the level once shared with Ireland.

Long gone are the days when England came to Dublin full of the old naivety and blessed with a few new caps. In 1987 (so near and yet so far away!) they came with two apprentice locks, Redman and Cusani, and a hospitable No. 8 called Simpson. Ireland won 17–0 and afterwards, at the post match dinner, treated the opposition with charm. We owed them a lot. Now, England

Who wants to stop us! Pat O'Hara leads a typical Irish charge with Phil Matthews, mouth open, giving vocal support against Wales.

travel with Dooley, Ackford and Richards. Ireland conceded 35 points at Twickenham in 1988, another 23 in 1990 and, suddenly, there is a gap where none had existed. The new Irish coach Ciaran Fitzgerald accepts as much: 'I have spoken about our current standing with the players. Our view is that the public sees us down there alongside Wales, behind England, France and Scotland. We believe that we can, in a short time, get to the same level as the French and Scots. But, we do accept that the gap between ourselves and England will be more difficult to close'.

Scotland's cleverness in moving with the winds of change, using them to freshen their game, has, perhaps, been the single most impressive achievement in Home Countries rugby over the last five seasons. Surely the Irish could do as their Celtic cousins have done? So far, it would seem not. Ireland recognises the changes, accepts the need to change but wants more time. Saint Augustine's fifth century prayer has a certain relevance to Irish rugby: 'Lord give me chastity – but not yet'.

Fitzgerald is expected to speed things up. Captain when Ireland won the Triple Crown in 1982, and skipper again when the Crown fell to his country in 1985, Fitzgerald commands respect. Not just from his players, not only from a fawning press but also, and most importantly, from the public. Beyond Ireland the memory may be of a brave and battered 1983 Lions skipper – a captain promoted beyond the level of his own competence – but at home the prophet is king. Our memory is of 'Fitzie', sleeves rolled to the elbows, headband wrapped around closely-cropped hair, screaming for one last charge. How could we forget the closing sequence to the 1985 Triple Crown decider against England. There was just a few minutes remaining, 10–9 to our dearest enemy and the prize was slipping away. There was a momentary pause in the game, the television camera picked up the Irish captain, as it did he was asking his last question, 'Where is your f. . . . . pride?' The No. 8 Brian Spillane, was moved sufficiently to leap on to an Irish drop out and stampede forward to get play to halfway. From there the team went further, forcing a line out deep inside English territory. Spillane's adrenalin still flowed at a rate of knots and up he went at the tail of the line, a direct tap to Lenihan on the peel, a charge, a ruck and Michael Kiernan's drop goal. Thirteen-ten to Ireland, no more questions from 'Fitzie'.

He came to the job in September 1990 with no coaching experience but he doesn't see that as a handicap: 'At this level how do you define the job? You are not there to improve people's skills, you wouldn't have time for that. You could spend twenty-four hours each day doing research on all the available players but I don't intend doing that either. I see the job more in terms of man-management and organisation. You identify the individual talents, try to get individual units within the side working and finally you hope to have all the

OPPOSITE: *Jim McCoy, one of Ireland's rugged prop-forwards, feeds the ball back despite the attentions of a New Zealand arm. Ireland have the ability to disrupt any opposition and have successfully rebuilt their team.*

OVERLEAF: *Martyn Morris, of Wales, attempts to stop another Irish surge. Ireland triumphed 14–8 in 1990 at Lansdowne Road and saved themselves from a whitewash.*

Donal Lenihan, one of the all time great Irish forwards, provides the rallying point against Wales. He missed the 1991 Five Nations championship through injury.

units working in unison.' It sounds quite a bit easier than it will be. But a few things are certain. Under Fitzgerald Ireland will be organised and combative. The man has an undeniable talent for commiting the uncommitted, for making lions out of the brave. There is a story from New Zealand rugby which pinpoints this intangible quality, this almost spiritual influence which the natural leader can exert.

On the night before the Ranfurly Shield match of 1959 between Auckland and Southland, the Auckland skipper Wilson Whineray went around each of his players saying there might come a time in the match when he would seek 'a supreme effort'. Albert Pryor, a Maori lock, described the effect on him of Whineray's request the next day: 'There was a break in the play and while we were standing in the lineout, waiting for the game to get going again, I heard Willie going up and down the line. "Supreme effort," he called out. "I want a supreme effort". I can never make anyone really understand what went on inside me when I heard those words. All I can say is that if Willie had come up to me and said "Albie, for the sake of the team, I want you to die." I would have died.'

Whatever else, Fitzgerald will send ripples across the well of pessimism. Dublin, at least on the morning of the Irish match, will be teeming with hope. One of rugby's great attractions is that a properly organised and highly motivated team can, occasionally, transcend the level of its own ability and beat a superior team.

According to the IRFU's Rugby Director, George Spotswood, there are approximately 45,000 playing the game in Ireland. Twenty thousand at schoolboy level, 10,000 at youth level and 15,000 playing adult rugby. It is a game of the middle class; an association which underlies the strength and weakness of Irish rugby. The consistently high level of organisation can hardly be a surprise given that committees are manned by captains of industry and pillars of local communities. When a club strays offside with its banker, it will turn to its own members. The bigger clubs can choose from a number of potential sponsors.

In their accounts for the end of the 1989–90 season the IRFU Committee could show to its members a credit balance of approximately £4.8 million (Irish punts). When it becomes possible to buy success Ireland will be up there, slugging it out with the best. In the interim, much will be invested in the redevelopment of Lansdowne which should be a floodlit, all-seater stadium before the turn of the century.

If impressive organisation and financial stability are the benefits of Irish rugby's place in the social order, there is a formidably negative side to the coin. The tentacles of Irish rugby do not extend into the smaller provincial towns, especially in the West of the country, and the game has no significant presence in the even smaller rural parishes. Amongst many citizens in rural Ireland, the sporting life begins and ends with gaelic football and hurling. These are perceived as the national pastimes and their status far transcends the mere attraction of the games. For too long there was an unspoken feeling that real Irishmen played gaelic games, that soccer and rugby were the foreign imports. For a country struggling in its search of an identity, these were important matters. Even if things have changed significantly over the last thirty years, traces of the old division still remain. What a pity that this should exist as rugby may be Ireland's most traditional sport.

There is evidence that it evolved from a ball game called Cad which was played by all branches of the Celtic race; Gaelic, British, Welsh, Cornish and Gallic. During the eighteenth century the game of Cad was dropped in Britain, largely through the influence of a number of prestigious public schools, including Rugby. It was replaced by the kicking game, later called soccer, whose rules were formulated by the Football Association in 1867. Ireland went on playing Cad and through the Irish influence the game was re-introduced in Britain. This happened, according to Fr Ferris, when an English boy, William Webb Ellis, learned the game from his cousins in Tipperary and later picked up the ball at Rugby School in 1823. Fr Ferris believed that Webb Ellis was, in fact, deciding to play Cad. Fr Ferris concluded a letter on the subject to the *Irish Times* in 1968 thus: 'Irish traditional football is Cad, now improperly called "Rugby". It would be a gracious act for the GAA (the governing body of gaelic games) to admit an error which has lasted only a lifetime and to restore the national game of Cad once more to its position of honour.'

A wishful thought! Time has washed away too many footprints for us to be sure of Rugby's origins and the game must make do with its place in the Irish scheme of things. Ciaran Fitzgerald insists that it will continue to suffer from its failure to penetrate some cultural and social barriers: 'The fellow that Irish rugby does not have access to is the one who has been brought up in a small rural parish, an environment where inter-parish rivalry has been the norm since his early childhood. We could do with his competitive mentality in Irish rugby.'

Neither does anyone believe that the essentially middle-class nature of the game in Ireland is helpful. Limerick alone stands as the city where rugby is truly the game of the people. Young Munster's supporters, bedecked in the black and amber of their favourites, leave their homes or local pub and walk to their home games at Greenfields. But, the reception for visiting teams has been far from lovely and, amongst the opposition, Greenfields is known as 'Killing Fields'.

It is rugby with passion. Graham Mourie's All Blacks lost just one match on their 1978 tour of Britain and Ireland and that was in Limerick. When the National League started at the beginning of the 1990–91 season, it was the Limerick clubs who set the competitive tone for what was to follow. If only their feeling for the game ran through every other Irish club. It doesn't. The more common attitude to the game is reflected in the confusion of the after-match dinner – such is the bonhomie, neutrals can rarely distinguish losers from winners.

The new league does threaten the old order and clubs like Shannon and Garrytown (both Limerick), Wanderers and Old Wesley (both Dublin), and the Ulster sides Ballymena and Instonians, are amongst those who have attracted major sponsorships and positively promoted a more professional approach. Others will follow. For their first three All Ireland League matches Wanderers collected £2,700 (Irish punts), £1,527 and £1,800 at the gate. After-match drinking in the bar yielded receipts of £3,200, £2,000 and £2,500 for the same three games. The spirit of the Irish game rises from the hearts of

If Ireland can find consistency at international level they will become a real force. McCoy provides another example of what the Irish love to do; crash forward causing mayhem.

those who play and spills from the hip flask of those who watch. Wanderers will know they are getting there when the receipts at the turnstiles far outstrip their bar takings.

If there are cultural hurdles to be cleared at adult level, there are no such difficulties in the schools. In the midst of the rugby recession the Irish Schools side could beat their English, Scottish and Welsh counterparts in the 1989–90 season. Since Ireland began competing at this level fifteen years ago, it has consistently matched and bettered its home country rivals. Blackrock College, for instance, standing on Dublin's fashionable South side, compares with any rugby school anywhere. Between Rock's primary school at Willow Park and the secondary school itself, around 1,000 pupils play the game and the best play it bloody well. Fergus Slattery, Brendan Mullin, Hugo MacNeill and Neil Francis may number amongst the more distinguished Rock graduates, but they are just four from a battalion. The schools game has long been a strong branch on the Irish tree, Charlie Haly and Rory Moloney, Oxford stars in the 1990 Varsity Match, learned the game at Presentation College Cork, another school which devotes time and thought to the production of rugby players. Mark Egan, the winning Oxford captain, came from Dublin's Terenure College.

But, maybe the greatest strength of Irish rugby is something of far greater importance than matches won and lost. The island of Ireland has been divided for almost seventy years and Northern Ireland has suffered enormously through the violence of the last twenty-five years. Where once there was tolerance, there is now intolerance. Irish rugby has managed to keep itself free of political chains and the team which represents Ireland represents every Irishman. To those beyond the island, that might not seem such a big deal. Well, I can tell you it is. Dublin, on the morning of a rugby international, is a flashing picture of an Ireland rarely experienced. Protestants from Ballymena, Catholics from Limerick and Dissenters from every county; all gathered together, sharing the same aspiration. And, if we can get a few points up, Catholic, Protestant and Dissenter will all sing together. *Molly Malone* becomes the true national anthem and for a few fleeting minutes the island of our dreams stands before us.

David Walsh is a rugby writer for the *Sunday Independent.*

Michael Kiernan, the Irish points scoring record breaker, is hoping to win back his place in the Irish team after being axed.

ITALY: The Italian squad;
they were winners of the European qualifying group.

ITALY

by
John Reason

When Italy began their attempt to qualify for the 1990 World Cup they seemed to have everything in their favour. All six matches were being played in the rugby heartland of Italy, a few miles from Venice. Their first match in September 1990 against Spain was in Rovigo, where first Carwyn James and now Naas Botha have built empires. Carwyn James did it as a coach and is revered for winning the Italian club championship for Rovigo. Naas Botha has done the same thing for Rovigo as a player. Rovigo, therefore, knows rugby as well as any place in Italy. So when Italy started against Spain as if they were schoolboys who had never played the game before, Rovigo let them know all about it. In particular, the *tiffosi* concentrated on making rude noises at the unfortunate Italian scrum-half Pietrosanti. It has to be said that he did not have the most penetrating of afternoons, and in that part of Italy it did not help his cause at all that he plays for a club in Rome.

Italy won, but not convincingly, and three days later they nearly lost to Holland in Treviso. The Dutch were comfortably the most engaging of the four national contestants, and because they had no choice in the matter they were comfortably the most amateur. Unfortunately, their playing aspirations did not reach much higher than a cheerful English Old Boys' team. For Italy to encounter real difficulty against them did not suggest that the rich patrons, busily pumping thousands of millions of lire into the game in Italy, are getting anything like value for money.

The crowd at Treviso thought the same. They also gave the bird to Bertrand Fourcade, Italy's French coach. He is said to have a three year contract worth £180,000. There was not much doubt that the customers did not think that they were getting value for money either. Rather in desperation, therefore,

Fourcade turned to a young man named Ivan Francescato to play scrum-half for Italy in the deciding game against Romania at Padua. It was Francescato's first game for Italy, and I am sure he will never forget it. Neither will all those who saw it. Francescato looks a bit like the young George Best: sharp, acquiline features, long black hair flying all over the place and the opposing defence in exactly the same sort of tangle. He really made Italy buzz and made the stadium at Padua roar. For some time, Romania's back row had not even resembled rusty lightening, never mind the greased variety, and neither had Gelu Ignat, the Romanian fly-half. Between the four of them, they did not even see the way Francescato went.

For the first time in any of the pool games Italy performed with style and purpose, and they played as if their national aspirations might amount to something more than a cavalcade of novices propped up by overseas stars. Mark Ella, the great Australian outside-half who is now helping to coach Milan, said after the match against Spain, 'Italy can play better than that.' He said the same after Italy's match against Holland, but we only stopped looking sceptical after Italy had beaten Romania. Italy owed that victory to Ivan Francescato, and the rude noises in Rovigo.

Italy played in the first Rugby World Cup in 1987 but achieved little in that

Italian scrum-half Pietrosanti makes the right decision by opting to get out of the way of England's giant lock, Bob Kimmins.

tournament. They did beat Fiji 18–15 and Marcello Cuttita scored one of the tries of the tournament, but New Zealand beat them by 70–6 in the first match of the World Cup. This defeat did nothing to dispel the perception that Italy's development as a rugby nation is being crippled by the top overseas players brought in to their clubs to bolster the street credibility of those Italian tycoons who have decided that a successful rugby team amounts to a significant status symbol in their own community. They certainly seem prepared to pay to get it, because it is alleged that the top two or three overseas players in Italy are being paid 200 million lire a year (£80,000) for which they are, naturally, prepared to put up with a few language difficulties in whatever nominal job they are supposed to be doing. Oddly enough the practice started when Umberto Marani, who is now a fine arts picture specialist with one of the leading London firms, developed his interest in rugby by taking some of the world's leading touring teams to play matches in his native country. No one could possibly be more faithful to the amateur ethic than Marani, so it is ironic that the philanthropic gesture he made all those years ago should have gestated the highest paid player market in the rugby world.

Now the process has got to the point where the Italian tycoons are so keen to add to the prestige they have established with their clubs that, where possible, they are encouraging overseas players to become naturalised Italians so that they can play for Italy. This option also enables Italian clubs to get around the present restriction of one overseas player per club. The Argentinian players now in Italy are being especially encouraged to take up this option. Apparently even David Campese, the Australian winger, could be eligible to play for Italy because of his Italian descent. In a strange way, this is bringing the history of Italian rugby full circle, because the game was first played in Italy back in 1910 between two clubs who were not Italian at all. The Racing Club of France and F.C. Servette of Geneva were invited to Turin by a group of Italian enthusiasts to demonstrate how the game should be played. Then British businessmen in Milan and Turin helped to get rugby started, but no sooner had they done so than the game fell into abeyance during the First World War.

It was not until 1926 that Stefano Bellandi and Piero Mariani managed to organise rugby teams in six major cities. Then, in 1928, the Italian Rugby Federation was formed and one year later Italy played their first international

Where Italy could have problems. Their tight forwards need to provide a platform for the talent behind the scrum.

match. It was against Spain, in a new stadium in Barcelona and, believe it or not, it was watched by a crowd of 80,000. Italy lost 9–0 but won the return match in Milan in 1930. Italy joined FIRA when France was banned from international rugby in the 1930s, and although Mussolini thought that the game would be good for Italian youth, Italy did not have much contact with rugby's mainstream until the early 1970s. The development of the game was then very rapid, with overseas players, and coaches like Roy Bish, Pierre Villepreux and Carwyn Jones, being imported. Much to the disquiet of the International Rugby Football Board, it soon became clear that overseas players were not going to Italy because they liked pasta or ice-cream. The circumstances of the importation had to be much more compelling than that.

For some reason – no one knows quite why – the disquiet felt by the International Board about the alleged breaches in the amateur regulations never developed into the anguish that led to France being cast into the outer

England's Neil Back is left facing four Italian defenders at Rovigo.

darkness forty years earlier. Perhaps it was because it was felt that rugby in Italy could not be taken as seriously as in France. Perhaps it was because Italy did not play against the Four Home Unions in an international championship.

Whatever the explanation, it still strikes some senior British rugby administrators as odd that out of more than thirty new countries who have been elected to the International Board, Italy should have been chosen as one of the four to be given a place on the Board's new executive committee. Romania were a bit miffed about this, for all sorts of reasons, but after Ivan Francescato had made sure that Italy would beat Romania and so finish top of their World Cup qualifying pool, their grumble sounded less convincing. Meanwhile, Francescato strolled away to ask the jostling and ingratiating tycoons to form an orderly queue and stop squabbling.

John Reason is rugby correspondent for the *Sunday Telegraph*.

JAPAN: The Japanese squad;
they were runners up in the Pacific qualifying group.

JAPAN

by
Austin Daniel

Japan's qualification for the 1991 World Cup brought huge sighs of relief from everyone involved in the financial side of the tournament. Not only would the Cup benefit from Japan's brand of running rugby, but their corporations would be easier to interest in the sponsorship packages. Japan provided the major sponsor for the 1987 World Cup and the yen will once again help the event move into the black. The strides will be massive rather than miniscule this time.

Japan have won through to join Scotland, Ireland and Zimbabwe and large sections of the Japanese population will watch every minute of the tournament. Television screens are to be erected in railway stations and other public places to satisfy the demand. Rugby is the most popular team sport in the country, with leading companies like Toyota and Nippon Steel continuing to propagate the game and the major universities providing a fertile nursery for players. At the last count there were 3,000 clubs, including schools, playing rugby. Shiggy Konno, who has been in charge of the game in Japan since the early 1960s, insists that figure could be even bigger. 'We could have many more than 80,000 players in the country had we sufficient playing fields to foster the sport to a much greater extent,' said Mr Konno.

Rugby first took a hold in the cities of Yokohama and Kobe in 1874 and then the Keio University indulged in the sport following the return to the country of Ginnosuke Tanaka who had attended Cambridge University. The presence at the turn of the century of Professor E.B. Clarke, who was in the faculty of history at Cambridge at the same time, was a tremendous boost for Tanaka. These two pioneers fostered the game and the first recorded match took place between Keio University and the exclusively British Yokohama Country and

Japan on the attack. The Japanese lack height in the forwards but possess international-class talent in the back division. Winning enough ball against top sides has been the recurring problem.

Athletic Club. This turned into an annual fixture and other clubs and schools followed suit. Keio Regatta and Athletic Club joined in the fixtures, and in 1911 Third High School in Keio added their name to the list. The school was helped by the Keio and Doshisha Universities to find matches and between 1911 and 1923 the game made steady progress.

The annual match between Keio and Doshisa universities has taken on the kind of importance that is associated with the Varsity Match between Oxford and Cambridge. In 1923 the Duke of Windsor was a spectator at a game played between Third High School and the Regatta club and three years later a milestone was achieved with the creation of the Japanese Rugby Football Union. The Second World War halted the growth of the game and a revival did not take place until 1952 when Oxford University toured Japan.

The JRFU was determined to move into the world of rugby and attacked this task with the kind of obsession that is so characteristic when the Japanese set their minds to achieving a goal. This is where Shiggy Konno has been such an important asset to the JRFU. He has carried his country's colours to the major rugby-playing nations and earned world renown at the same time. The Four Home Unions, France, Canada, USA, New Zealand and Australia, have all played host to the red-and-cherry-hooped players who wear the chrysanthemum as an emblem.

Konno believes that despite Japan's large pool of players their style of play and tactics are not as successful now as in the 1970s when Japan caused a stir around the globe with their lively rugby. South Korea, their arch rivals, have in the late 1980s closed the gap and recorded victories over Japan in 1986, 1988 and 1989. Although Japan can boast eight Asia rugby titles the Koreans have now captured four. With the next tournament to be held in Seoul in 1992, that gap is likely to get smaller.

Japan had the satisfaction of qualifying for this World Cup and Ichiro Isoda, the JRFU president, is not disheartened by Japan's most recent showings against the Koreans. Isoda predicts his country will make a big impact in the 1991 Cup and took heart from the team's performance in 1990 against the American Eagles, despite a 25–15 loss. The Japanese under-23 team clipped the Eagles' wings 16–0 in Nagoya and the majority of that young side will be in the World Cup squad. They will be coached by Hiroshi Shukuzawa, a former test scrum-half in the 1970s.

The squad will be captained by Seiji Hirao, who has won more than twenty caps for his country and who performed with distinction in the 1987 World Cup. Seasoned lock-forward Atushi 'Jumbo' Oyagi will be winding up his international career in this tournament. The 29-year-old is joined in the second row by one of two non-Japanese members of their Cup squad, the Western Samoan E. Luaiufi; while there is a Tongan, Senevi Latu in the back row. They will help Japan make their mark on this tournament.

Austin Daniel is a freelance rugby writer.

NEW ZEALAND: The New Zealand squad; they are the 1987 World Cup champions.

NEW ZEALAND

by
T.P. McLean

New Zealanders, at home and abroad, took considerable comfort from the two test wins achieved by the All Blacks in France in 1990. Those victories proved the 1987 World Cup champions were once again a dominant force. Grant Fox, the All Black outside-half, kicked magnificently and took his international points total past 400.

However, not all Kiwis took the view that everything was back on course. The All Blacks had set off for France having lost their 50 game unbeaten run to Australia who had come back to win the third test of the series in New Zealand. Scotland had already completed their series against the All Blacks and had been unlucky to lose the second and final test 21–18. The French tour produced two defeats for the All Blacks, against French Selection XVs, and Kiwis were thoughtfully scraping their jaws.

Former players and coaches had, it must be said, for some time been discussing the tactics of the current All Blacks. Bob Stuart, a former test captain, witnessed the 1989 All Blacks clash with the Barbarians at Twickenham. He said, 'For ten minutes just after half time the Barbarians had the winning of the game. It was a near thing before Wayne Shelford (the All Black captain) regained control and it seemed to me that flaws might be developing in the All Black machine.'

At the same time Kiwis of comparable stature began uttering what could have been called heretical statements, considering the extraordinary All Black record since their defeat by France in Nantes in 1986. Former All Black full-back Bob Scott said, 'I will not be troubled to pay $NZ 33 for a test match seat at Eden Park. At every recent test I have attended I have waited for "real" rugby to begin. It never does. I can't be bothered watching wing-forwards

Richard Loe helping the Barbarians against England in 1990. The New Zealand prop is a key figure in the All Black scrum and is effective in the loose.

maul and ruck all over the field until Fox kicks the goals. Nothing else happens. Test rugby? Test baloney!'

When Scotland arrived for their 1990 series Alex Wyllie, the coach, announced that Shelford, the reigning captain, had been dropped. He said the decision followed anxieties about Shelford's physical state. The implication that a fit again Shelford would be recalled was not substantiated by later events. Public disquiet at the departure of Shelford was considerable. This ardent, even ferocious-looking man, who had led the All Blacks on so many charges, had clout, persona and appeal. This was measured by the success of his autobiography with 20,000 copies sold in two weeks and a second run of 5,000 went just as quickly. The Kiwi public sorrowed for 'Buck', as he is known throughout the game.

As the 1990 season unfolded the suspicions of Stuart were followed by the

Such strength and speed is too much for opponents all over the rugby world. John Kirwan is a continuing threat on the All Black right wing.

criticisms of more ex-All Blacks with the mid-field tactics being described by one as 'boring'. It could be argued that New Zealand rugby had suffered four catastrophic blows during the 1980s which all played their part in creating the atmosphere that existed in 1990.

First there was the tour, in 1981, by a Springbok team to New Zealand. Civic disorder developed and bloody clashes were fought between police and demonstrators against apartheid. Friendships and even families, were torn apart in the violence of protest. At Auckland Grammar, one of the great bastions of schools' rugby, more pupils in 1982 played Association football than played rugby football. When, by legal injunction upheld by the Privy Council, the New Zealand Rugby Union in 1985 was barred from sending the All Blacks to South Africa, most members of the team, amid secrecy rivalling that which cloaked the development of Kerry Packer's World Series Cricket

circus, joined together to tour as the Cavaliers. They were officially disowned by the New Zealand Union and were punished by being dropped for two internationals. Each Cavalier swore that, beyond the agreed daily allowance of the International Board, he had not recieved a penny. A ringleader, Andy Haden, in a book later revealed that, with the connivance of the South African Board, very substantial sums had been paid by Yellow Pages and other sponsors into a team fund. The yield from this was later said to be at least $NZ100,000 a man tax-free. Nothing could be done by the New Zealand Union. Team funds have become sacrosanct to each All Black tour.

Soon after the Cavaliers' tour, commercialism became the ardent practice of a number of leading players. John Kirwan, as the sole employee of a company devoted to promotional and entrepreneurial activities, drove about Auckland in a car bearing his name. Shelford was hired by the International Management Group, and was engaged in all sorts of public activities, starting with speaking engagements. The fees charged for his appearances were considerable.

The final blow to what had been, for more than 120 years, the national pastime, the game of the people, the sport which most young Kiwis played in the true spirit of amateurism, was the sudden rush, in early 1990, of a number of leading players into professional rugby league in either England or Australia. John Gallagher, a full-back of great attacking and limited defensive powers, was signed by Leeds. Matthew Ridge, went to Manly with John Schuster, an outstanding midfield-back; Brett Iti, an Auckland scrum-half rated by Freddie Allen as the best in the country and Darryl Halligan, a full-back of exemplary promise, both left rugby union as well.

There was also the declaration to Ridge by 600 Maoris of Kaitaia, hitherto for generations as devoted to rugby union as to a religious cause, that they would switch to league. This devastating thrust demonstrated how solidly, with the powerful aid of television, league had awakened public interest. Eddie

OPPOSITE: Jonathan Davies, formerly of Wales and now in rugby league, crashes into John Kirwan. The winger's determination is plainly obvious.

OVERLEAF: It's at times like this you want to shout 'yours'! Wales's Paul Thorburn has the job of standing up to Steve McDowell and a whole army of All Blacks.

Terry Wright has electric speed but Tony Underwood, for the Barbarians, managed to prevent a try this time. Wright will need to be closely watched in the World Cup.

Tonks, successor to Russell Thomas as NZ RFU chairman, was soon expressing his concern about the popularity of league. The consolation, that a tour of New Zealand by the Great Britain league team attracted desperately poor houses at considerable cost to the British league, was not remarked. Yet, there was little doubt that the rush of players into the said game could be attributed not only to the substantial cash offerings but also to a much wider public appreciation of the game.

So, marching towards the defence of the Webb Ellis Cup and facing the formidable challenge of England in the first match, New Zealand rugby has not been firing on all cylinders. If the selectors, who had been proven conservative in their evaluation of young and/or promising players, continued not to notice that some of the First XV had marched over the crest, the day when their teams could not expect victory as of right might be just around the corner.

The prospect scarcely pleased. Since a 19-year-old New Zealander, Charles John Monro, returning in 1870 from schooling in Christ's College in the London suburb of Finchley, had persuaded young men and schoolboys to take to the newfangled game of rugby in which he had been trained, the country, Maori and White, had eagerly embraced the sport. By 1888, a British team captained by one of England's great all-rounders, A.E. Stoddart, had toured the Colony, scoring 13 wins in a programme of nineteen matches. No sooner was this tour over than a former Blackheath man, Thomas Eyton, and a Maori of substance, Joe Warbrick, brought together twenty-six men, four of them White, the rest Maori, for a tour which embraced 107 matches and which lasted for more than a year.

Australia and New Zealand had been exchanging visits since the early 1880s. In 1903, at Sydney, New Zealand beat Australia in the first official international to be played Down Under. Much more importantly, in 1904, New Zealand, not yet known as the All Blacks, defeated a British team skippered by a Scot, 'Darkie' Bedell-Sivright, by 9 points to 3 in the first international to be played on a New Zealand field. In no time, New Zealand was accepting an invitation to despatch a team on a prolonged tour of the British Isles, internationals to be played against each of the Four Home Unions.

The consequences were extraordinary. The New Zealanders who, soon after the start of the tour, were christened 'All Blacks', had won twenty-seven matches before, at Cardiff Arms Park, they succumbed to Wales by 0–3 in a match forever coloured by a dispute about the refusal of a 27-year-old Scottish referee, John Dallas, to award an All Black centre named Robert Deans a try which he and his teammates claimed had been fairly scored. The All Blacks' captain, David Gallaher, who was to be killed by shrapnel in the Battle of

Passchendaele in 1917, graciously said the Welsh had been the better team. His countrymen disapproved. Their team had been cheated.

It mattered not. What mattered was that the team carried on to a record, in the British Isles, of thirty-one victories and one loss and an extraordinary points record of 830 scored against no more than 39 yielded. As if influenced by a powerful drug, New Zealanders, whatever their age, whatever their sex, whatever their race, were consumed by a pride in the performances, year after year, all around the world, against all manner of opponents, of their wonderful All Blacks. The Second All Blacks who toured in England, Ireland, Wales and

OPPOSITE: *Joe Stanley, the All Black centre, is held by Phil Matthews (left) and David Irwin against Ireland. Gary Whetton arrives to support the strong running Stanley.*

ABOVE: *Nick Farr-Jones, the Australian captain, is pursued by the All Blacks back row in the 1989 contest with the Barbarians.*

All Black lock Murray Pierce leaps high for possession against Wales. Buck Shelford (headband) looks to win the loose ball.

France in 1924 became The Invincibles because they were unbeaten in thirty-two matches, including two in France and two in Canada. Scotland opted out of this tour because of grievances dating back to 1905 and centring principally on the payment of a trifling daily tour allowance to the All Blacks.

Rugby was *the* national game and at most colleges and secondary schools, it could be avoided as a compulsory exercise only by the production of a medical certificate. With time, and an expanding population, the country of about 109,000 square miles became divided into twenty-seven provinces affiliated to the New Zealand Union. In each of these, club competitions were spiritedly fought until it was time for the representative sides to meet each other in ten or a dozen matches in a season. A trophy was presented by a Governor of the Colony, the Earl of Ranfurly, in the first years of the twentieth century.

Maoris and 'Pakehas', as the Whites were called, played in harmony. A 19-year-old Maori full-back named George Nepia, by playing in every one of the 'Invincibles' matches, was immortalised before he had reached voting age; and before his death, aged 81, he had become the first 'black' (Maoris are a brown-raced people), ever to be elected as an honorary life vice-president of the South African Rugby Board.

The triumphs (and some disappointments, even disasters) went on and on. Until the decade of the 1980s, when the Springboks toured New Zealand, the Cavaliers toured South Africa, quasi-professionalism was embraced by some fine players and a rush began into the gold mines of rugby league, the game was a pleasure, a pursuit, a princely activity. Even amid the difficulties of the 1980s, the All Blacks were formed into a team of irresistible strength and quite astonishing physical fitness. Thus the first World Cup tournament was won with one scientific slaughter after another.

Now, the question being asked is: were those ten minutes after half-time in the Baa-Baas match at Twickenham in 1989 a warning that, in 1991, New Zealand rugby might be engaged in a mighty struggle to retain the World Cup?

T.P. McLean is New Zealand's most renowned rugby journalist.

ROMANIA: *The Romanian squad;*
they were runners up in the European qualifying tournament.

ROMANIA

by
John Reason

When Romania beat France in Bucharest in 1960, their rugby was accorded the recognition it had craved ever since their university students had come back home from Paris and London to start playing the game before the First World War.

After that match France offered Romania an annual fixture, and that led to Romania's development as a significant force in European rugby. It had taken Romania fifty years to make the breakthrough.

The first Rugby clubs were founded in Bucharest between 1910 and 1912 and were usually sections added to clubs which were originally formed to play other sports, such as the Tennis Club Roman. Romania lost no time in forming a national Rugby Federation. Back in the nineteenth century it had taken between thirty and forty years for Rugby football to be identified with a national organisation in England. It took only two years in Romania. The Romanian Rugby Federation was formed in 1912. Two years after that, they organised their first national club championships. The winners were Tennis Club Roman. They won the championship for the next two years, and again in 1917 and 1918.

The following year, Romania played their first international match in Paris, but surprisingly, it was not against France. It was played against the USA, and America won 21–0. Romania explained carefully to their French hosts that the game was only a friendly! Six years later, France would have been glad to avail themselves of the same excuse when they took part in the rugby tournament which for the first time, and so far for the only time, was included as part of the Olympic Games. There were only three teams in the tournament in Paris because the British teams loftily declined to enter, and although France beat

Cristian Raducanu, the Romanian forward, wins the ball ahead of Scotland's Derek White at Murrayfield. The Romanians will be aiming to make a bigger impression at this second World Cup.

Romania by 59–3, they also lost to the USA. There was no argument about it, either. The USA beat France 17–3 at Stade Colombes, and therefore have been the Olympic champions of Rugby football ever since, because Rugby football has never been played again as an Olympic sport.

Romanian rugby has always been glad of its French connection, just like the country of Romania itself. For most of this century, Romania has been almost a province of France, just as it once was a province of Rome. Romania's towns and cities have the architecture of provincial France. They smell like provincial France, all garlic and Gauloise, and until comparatively recently, when the English language took over, French was the second language of the middle classes.

The combination of modern Paris and ancient Rome gives Romania and its rugby unlimited potential, providing the game is taught in the schools. Those of us who had only seen Romania under the yoke of a cynically nepotistic Communist dictatorship always felt that if only the country could throw off that appalling burden, it could become a paradise both for tourists and rugby players.

After all, the place has a Roman history. A Black Sea coast. It is self-sufficient in agriculture and in oil. It grows its own wine. It has hot, Mediterranean summers and cold, snowy winters where Count Dracula learned to ski in Translyvania. It has some of the most beautiful women in Europe. Its caviar is the best in Europe.

If only Romania could gain its freedom, we said, within five years, it could leave Nice and Juan les Pins for dead. Now, it looks as if that might happen. Romania has largely gained its freedom, though sadly at a terrible cost in human life. The world would like to believe that the revolutions in Eastern Europe in 1989 were born of the people, but whether they were or not, the fact is that men like Florica Murariu died.

Murariu had captained Romania at rugby football. A dynamic flanker, he had been part of Romania's greatest international successes. He had played in the 13–13 draw against Ireland at Lansdowne Road in 1980. He had played in the 24–6 demolition of Wales in 1983 and he had played in the 28–22 defeat of Scotland in 1984. He captained the Romanian team that beat Wales 15–9 in Cardiff in 1988, too, and even after their victory he was still sore about the match he had played as a young man in Cardiff ten years earlier, when Wales had snatched a 13–12 victory at the last gasp with a stratagem that Romania will always feel was unfair. Romania were leading 12–10 at the end and their full-back, Bucos, made a mark. All he had to do was kick to touch and Romania would win. Before Bucos could take the kick, Bobby Windsor charged. Bucos clearly felt that Windsor should not have been allowed to do that, and he hesitated, looking at referee Palmade from France. The referee made no attempt to intervene, so Bucos, badly flustered, took a tapped kick. Palmade promptly blew his whistle and said that the kick had not gone through the mark. Wales were given a scrum, and from it, Gareth Davies dropped the winning goal. Most definitely, justice was not done.

In 1989, a year after Romania had gained their 15–9 win in Cardiff through the explosive kicking of Gelu Ignat, Florica Murariu was shot dead, killed by a panicking young soldier in the revolution. The following Spring, the rugby players of the rest of Europe paid tribute to the memory of Murariu and all the others who had died. A match was played at Twickenham to raise funds both for Romanian charities and for Romanian rugby.

Those who knew Romania, knew how much hope the future held for both the country and for the game of rugby in that country. Some of them also knew how much Romanian rugby owed to France, and to those Romanian players who, on that famous day in Bucharest in 1960, had beaten France for the first time. The score, in the days of the three point try, was 11–5. Again, no argument. It was a powerful French team, too, with Michel Vannier at full-back, with Guy Boniface and Jackie Bouquet in the centre, with Lacroix and Albaladejo at half-back, and with Domenech, Mommejat, Crauste, Celaya and Moncla in the pack. Romanian rugby had arrived.

Since then, Romania has given nearly all the top International Board countries hard games, including New Zealand, but perhaps Romania's greatest performance was in 1980, three days after they had drawn with Ireland. They went to Leicester, and played against the strongest club side in England. A side containing players of the calibre of 'Dusty' Hare, Paul Dodge, Clive Woodward and Les Cusworth. A side that had made the John Player Cup its own property. Romania were not impressed. They were not even concerned. They played so marvellously well that those rueful Leicester Tigers are still trying to work out what him them. Within ten minutes, Romania had scored three times, and they went on to win 39–7. No argument about that, either. Florica Murariu scored four tries himself, and Ion Constantin, their goalkicker, once kicked the ball right out of the Leicester ground. That night, Leicester had an uncomfortable feeling that the ionosphere was named after Constantin.

To this day, Romania have always produced beautiful kickers, and thanks to the influence and the encouragement of France, they have almost always had sharp, thrusting hookers, top class scrum-halves, and loose forwards to rival those from New Zealand. That night at Leicester, Romania had all four. Munteanu was a dynamo, Constantin kicked the dead ball like a shell, Alexandru drop-kicked it almost as far, Paraschiv was in his bustling element at scrum-half, and Marariu, Bors and Stoica came off the back of the scrum and the back of the lineout like Panzers. French it may have been, but still unforgettable.

The privations that caused the 1989 revolution led to desperately hard times for rugby too. Romania's venture in the first World Cup, in 1987, was not a success. They lost heavily to France and to Scotland and only beat Zimbabwe by a single point. Still, they qualified comfortably for the 1991 World Cup, and they are delighted that they will be playing their pool matches in France, because some of their players play for French clubs, and a lot more would like to. This cross-fertilisation with France has helped Romania in the past, and under the presidency of Viorel Moraru, formerly one of Romania's greatest flankers, and the guidance of Radu Demian, their secretary, and Valeriu Irimescu – both great players, too – Romania are rebuilding for the future.

They are also exploring the whole wide world of rugby football for the first time. No country will have played more matches, or travelled further, in their preparation for the 1991 World Cup than Romania.

John Reason is the rugby correspondent of the *Sunday Telegraph*.

Romania 15 Wales 19; the famous scoreline for Romanian rugby achieved at Cardiff in 1988 and an example of why they defeated the Welsh.

SCOTLAND: *The Scotland squad;*

they qualified by right for the World Cup finals.

SCOTLAND

by
Peter Donald

Concentration, continuity and commitment could be classed as the three main ingredients which enable Scotland to compete with, and often beat, much bigger nations in terms of rugby population. They foster the belief that, in the second World Cup tournament, the Scottish team will fare at least as well and possibly better than they did four years ago, when they reached the quarter-finals. The three 'Cs' are simply explained. Being a relatively small nation, Scotland's top players are concentrated mainly in the first division of a tight and well-organised league structure, although when naming an international team, the selectorial net is cast a little wider to incorporate Scots who may be playing, through force of circumstances, outside the country's boundaries. In the 1989–90 season, for example, the team that won the Grand Slam was drawn from ten of the fourteen clubs who constitute the first of the seven divisions in the McEwan's league, with London Scottish contributing three players and Bath and Nottingham one each.

Continuity is an essential factor and the Scottish Rugby Union has established an ideal framework which ensures that few young players of real promise escape official notice. The groundwork, of course, begins at the schools. In Scotland there are around 11,000 boys playing the game and the best are carefully groomed through inter-district matches and internationals at under-15 and under-18 age levels. From school they progress to a similar junior and senior framework in the clubs, of which Scotland has approximately 260 encompassing between 13,000 and 14,000 players. Again, the best come through to compete at under-18 and under-21 age levels for their districts and their country.

The coaching throughout is intense and carefully monitored in order to produce a Scottish style of play. It is this commitment to a common theme in the rugby education of players which ensures that those who go on to play for their country are ready for the challenge and the final examination of their capabilities. This in turn makes the coach's task easier and again continuity has been a vital factor in helping Scotland to achieve two Grand Slams in the space of seven years.

Jim Telfer of Melrose, a former Scotland and British Lions forward who also coached the Lions, was in charge of the 1984 Grand Slam team and he is still lending his invaluable experience as assistant to Ian McGeechan of Headingley, who coached the squad that won all their matches in the 1989–90 season. Telfer maintained that the seeds of the 1984 triumph were sewn in the summer tours of New Zealand and Australia in 1981 and 1982. Most of the players who participated in those tours were there to carry the lessons they had

BELOW: *Gary Armstrong displays the form that has made him such a crucial member of Scotland's World Cup plans. His strength and commitment give the Scots an extra back-row forward.*

OPPOSITE: *The White Shark! John Jeffrey is heading for a fall against Wales as his search for the ball gets him into a highly unusual position.*

learned and the team spirit they had developed into the Grand Slam of 1984.

A momentary lapse in continuity was suitably punished the following season when Jim Aitken, the Gala prop who had captained Scotland to their triumphant run the previous year, was dropped and other changes were made. From their position at the top of the table, the Scots slipped to the bottom and Aitken, understandably aggrieved at the way he had been cast aside, issued a timely warning that a team riding high must not take things for granted. The slightest lapse in concentration, commitment and continuity can prove costly.

Scotland, however, clawed their way back from that disappointment and rose to the top again in a creditably short space of time. McGeechan was the 'pilot' and the Yorkshireman who, like Telfer, had gained international honours with Scotland and the British Lions and coached the Lions on their highly successful tour to Australia in 1989, followed up 1990's run in the home internationals by taking Scotland on tour to New Zealand during the summer,

when they came so close to beating the All Blacks in the second test.

For the first time on a major tour, Scotland did not lose a non-international match. They opened up by crushing a Poverty Bay/East coast side 45–0, drew 16–all with a powerful Wellington team and, after beating Nelson Bays/ Marlborough 23–6, set themselves up for the first Test with an encouraging 21–12 win over Canterbury followed by a sweeping 45–12 result against Southland.

After such a promising run, the test at Carisbrook was a bitter disappointment for the Scots. Lacking strength in the middle of the lineout, they went down to a convincing defeat. Although they led twice in the first half at 6–3 and 10–9 with centre Sean Lineen, the New Zealand-born Scot scoring his first international try, the second half went against them, particularly at the lineout, where Ian Jones was a dominant figure for the All Blacks. New Zealand built up a 31–10 lead before the Scots rallied in the closing stages with a try by skipper David Sole from a short penalty. The 31–16 defeat did not, however, take the heart out of the tour party. They went on to register a 19–4 midweek win over Manawatu and then surprised their hosts with a tremendous challenge in the second Test at Eden Park, Auckland.

It may be an over-simplification to suggest that if Grant Fox had not been in such superb form with his goal-kicking Scotland might have won, but the fact remains that Fox scored all but four of New Zealand's points with five penalty goals and a conversion in a 21–18 win, whereas the Scots won the try-count by two to one with wingers Tony Stanger and Alex Moore, on his international debut, both crossing the All Blacks' line.

McGeechan described it as 'an encouraging tour', and it was a remarkable achievement made possible by astute coaching and supreme team-work. All the players who had featured in the Grand Slam made themselves available for the tour and the selectors were also able to give invaluable experience to

OPPOSITE: *Sean Lineen, the New Zealander who has become an integral part of Scotland's back division, is outjumped by Serge Blanco, of France.*

OVERLEAF: *Scotland captain David Sole has developed into a world-class forward and inspiring leader. His ability to make considerable ground from line outs and mauls causes major problems for the opposition.*

several promising young players, three of whom were drawn from Jim Telfer's Melrose club; George 'Doddie' Weir, a 6ft 7in lock forward, Graham Shiel, a stand-off or centre, and Craig Redpath, a centre or full-back. All three players, like their clubmate Craig Chalmers, the Scotland stand-off, are products of the Scottish Rugby Union's youth development programme but it could be said that the general improvement of the game in Scotland goes back to the introduction of official league rugby in the 1973–74 season.

There are currently ninety-eight clubs making up seven divisions in the league, and it is an indication of the success and popularity of the system that the sponsorship has changed only once in eighteen years. Promotion and relegation enable clubs to improve their fixture lists and give their players the chance to reach the higher stratas of representative rugby. Three clubs, for example, have managed to climb from the bottom division to the top. Highland from Inverness were the first, although their stay in Division One was brief and they have slipped back. But, it was important that their players were given a taste of rugby at the top. Currie, a club based on the outskirst of Edinburgh, has achieved first division status but the most successful outfit has undoubtedly been Stirling County, who were in Division Seven thirteen years ago and have shown impressive form in Division One. Much of their success has been due to the development of a strong youth section in which mini and midi tournaments have attracted youngsters and kept them involved and coached in the basics of the game until they were ready to graduate through to fifteen-a-side rugby.

Stirling County's success has enabled them to attract players who might otherwise have gravitated to some of the top clubs in the Glasgow or Edinburgh areas, most of whom have now loosened their school former pupil restrictions and opened their doors in a limited way to outsiders. This growth in semi–open clubs has resulted in the country's best players joining teams who are playing their rugby in Division One although there are occasional complaints from the smaller clubs about this drain on their resources.

Inevitably, the structure of the league has come in for periodic criticism. While the clubs who for the most part find themselves struggling to stay clear

David Sole, with his trade-mark headband, will be one of the leading figures in this year's World Cup competition.

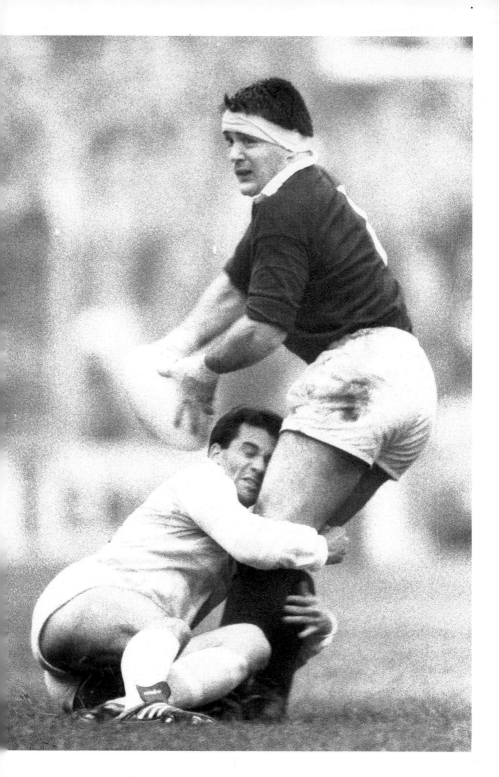

of relegation are quite content to maintain a set-up involving fourteen clubs in each division, some near the top of Division One favour a reduction in the numbers to, say, eight teams playing each other on a home and away basis. Until now the teams have met only once in a season on league business. It is felt that a home and away arrangement involving the strongest teams would make the league games more intensely competitive and give the top players better preparation for international rugby. On the other hand, it is argued that such a programme might put too great a strain on the players, requiring them to produce peak performances each week with no intervening games of less pressure. Occasional attempts to reorganise the system and produce a smaller top division have failed to find the necessary support and now attention is being focussed on the introduction of a national knock-out competition in addition to the league championship.

Knock-out tournaments have been staged for some years but mainly on a regional basis in the various Scottish districts. There is widespread support, however, for a national event, the closing rounds of which would help to fill the present void in the last few weeks of the season, which are dominated by seven-a-side tournaments across the country. The problem is finding time in an already crowded calendar for the preliminary rounds and, indeed, for days in the closing weeks which would not clash with popular 'sevens' events, particularly those in the Border country. Beginning on the first Saturday in April, Gala, Melrose, Hawick, Jedforest and Langholm have traditionally staged their 'sevens' on the final five Saturdays of the season. It is mainly these clubs who are wary of the introduction of a national knock-out event and the effect it might have on their tournaments which, they maintain, are essential to their finances. It is hoped, however, that once the World Cup has been completed the Scottish Rugby Union will present a format which will be

OPPOSITE: *Sean Lineen loses the ball as the French mid-field closes in on the Scotland centre in Paris. Scotland's own defence continues to impress at international level.*

BELOW: *John Jeffrey uses a sliding tackle to stop the ball falling into Argentinian hands. Arbizu is the Argentine player left groping for possession.*

acceptable to all clubs and enable a further level to be added to the competitive scene in the country.

While the club league structure has improved the standard of competition generally, the competition closest to the hearts of the international selectors is the Scottish District Championship, which is also sponsored by McEwan's and which embraces five teams, Edinburgh, Glasgow, the South of Scotland, the North and Midlands, and the Anglo-Scots. The ten games involving these five sides are generally compressed into the last five Saturdays of the calendar year and are confidently expected to bring together the best players in the country. The competition began as long ago as 1953 but it is only recently that the Anglo-Scots have been full participants.

For many years it was accepted that the strength of Scottish rugby was concentrated in the Borders, whose senior clubs have often provided the framework of the national side. As in Wales, rugby comes ahead of football as the main winter sport in the Borders, whereas the round ball game dominates the sporting scene in other parts of the country. It could still be said that the Borders are the main force in the game, with six of their seven senior teams in Division One and the club championship having only once gone outside the district in the first seventeen years of the competition. That was in 1979, when Heriot's F.P. took the title to Edinburgh and brought to an end a run of five consecutive Hawick victories. Hawick, however, came back to claim five more wins and their record puts them far ahead of the other Border challengers, such as Gala with three successes, Kelso with two and Melrose with one. While the division title has been dominated by Border clubs, there has been a growing challenge from teams in Edinburgh and the West, notably Boroughmuir, Heriot's F.P., Edinburgh Academicals, Glasgow High/Kelvinside and, of course, Stirling County.

The District Championship has not proved quite such a dominant scene for the Border clubs, who contribute to the South of Scotland XV. The South still lead the way but Edinburgh are not far behind and the Anglo-Scots are a growing force in this event. There have been calls to disband the District Championship and release players for more club games but as long as the national selectors place so much reliance on this competition as a 'stepping stone' to higher achievements there is little chance of that happening. Indeed, some players and officials would like to see the district format being extended

Ready for action. The Scotland front row of Paul Burnell, Kenny Milne and captain David Sole (headband) prepare for another scrum.

so that the five Scottish teams could play regular representative against English and Welsh opposition.

Injuries, of course, can seriously affect the prospects of any team and Scotland is particularly vulnerable in this respect, with fewer players of true international class at its disposal. The ability of the key men to steer clear of injury can be a vital success factor, as was demonstrated in the 1990 Grand

Slam campaign when the Scots went through all four matches using only sixteen players; even including the early-season victories over Fiji and Romania the total was only twenty. In the last World Cup, on the other hand, there was a damaging blow to Scotland's hopes when that superlative tactician, John Rutherford, one of the best stand-off halves in the game, was an early casualty with a knee injury and had to be flown home. There was no one of comparative class to take his place and it says much for the rest of the players and their teamwork that, even without Rutherford, they managed to reach the quarter-finals. They might indeed have gone further had they not come up against the eventual winners, New Zealand, at that stage of the competition. The All Blacks conceded that Scotland gave them one of their hardest games, a view that was strengthened when the Scots came so close to beating New Zealand in the second test last year.

Another international championship and a close season tour to the United States and Canada have passed since that visit to New Zealand but the team spirit developed throughout the splendid achievements of 1990 are still there. More importantly so are most of the players. While the All Blacks have suffered losses to rugby league, as indeed have Wales, Scotland have so far escaped that drain on their resources. Only Finlay Calder, the Stewart's-Melville F.P. flanker who captained the victorious British Lions in Australia in 1989, has decided that he has finished with international rugby and, while there is no shortage of candidates for his position, his influence both on and off the field will be missed. Although he stepped down from the captaincy in 1989 to make way for David Sole, Calder's presence in the team was still an inspiration to the men around him. Roy Laidlaw, Scotland's record breaking scrum-half with forty-seven caps to his credit, shared in the 1984 Grand Slam and took part in the last World Cup. He believes that Calder's personality and experience could make him a useful addition to Scotland's strike force, if only as a father figure and morale booster to the shadow squad who will be standing by in case of injuries.

Ian McGeechan, of course, already has an able and experienced team of coaches alongside him, with Jim Telfer, his assistant, taking charge of the forwards and two first class back-up men in Derrick Grant of Hawick and Douglas Morgan of Stewart's-Melville F.P. All served their time as international players and have now worked together for almost two years. This

TOP: *Buck Shelford, of New Zealand, finds a way of keeping Serge Blanco, the French full-back, quiet in the 1987 World Cup final.*

BOTTOM: *The famous New Zealand 'haka' with the stadium at Nantes providing the background for this special picture.*

OVERLEAF: *Gary Whetton (New Zealand) is wrapped up by the long arms of Olivier Roumat, the French lock-forward.*

OPPOSITE: *Australia's Michael Lynagh showing the form that has made him the greatest points scorer the game has seen.*
ABOVE: *A perfect throw and a perfect leap. Olivier Roumat gets his fingertips to the ball against the All Blacks.*
LEFT: *Paul Thorburn, the Welsh captain, puts his heart and soul into the national anthem.*
OVERLEAF: *England's Jeff Probyn (centre) destroys an Argentine line out.*

OPPOSITE: Ireland's Donal Lenihan asks for more from his team. All Irishman will be hoping to see Lenihan in the starting line up for the World Cup after his injury problems.

team of four was appointed to take Scotland through to the end of the World Cup campaign. It is another example of the continuity which the Scottish Rugby Union has sought to establish and which, to date, has served the game well. McGeechan, Telfer, Grant and Morgan have built up a keen rapport with the squad of players from whom the likely World Cup representatives will be chosen. Three members of the coaching team are also on the international selection committee, with Telfer having a standing invitation to join in deliberations at any time. It is a sensible and broadminded arrangement which gives Scotland the benefit of the views of the top men in the game, men who are also closely associated with the players at club and district level.

Scotland have been lucky with the draw for the World Cup on this occasion. They are initially in Pool Two along with Japan, Zimbabwe and Ireland. All of these games involving Scotland will be played at Murrayfield, which undoubtedly gives the Scots a big advantage. Should they win their Pool they will then come up against the runners-up in Pool three, comprising Australia, Wales, Argentina and Western Samoa and that match is also scheduled for Murrayfield, as is the semi-final involving the winners from the above two Pools. This means that a good run in the opening rounds of the competition could find Scotland appearing in five internationals on their own ground between 5 October and 26 October. It is an exciting prospect for the home team and its supporters, although such an intense programme of matches will clearly strain the Scottish squad's resources to the full, even if the top players do manage to steer clear of injuries.

Being together on home territory for three weeks has obvious advantages in that replacements are within easy call, but it could also present certain problems. Squad training sessions and matches will occupy only about half of the time and it will be up to the coaches to keep the players involved in other activities during the 'rest' periods.

Peter Donald is the *Daily Telegraph* rugby correspondent in Scotland.

USA: The USA squad;

they were third in the America's qualifying tournament.

UNITED STATES OF AMERICA

by
Peter McMullan

The United States of America Rugby Football Union was only established in 1975, yet the Americans are taking part in their second World Cup. This fact is an indication of the potential existing in a country that is, by the standards of the Four Home Unions and other rugby nations, still in its infancy. What will happen when the child grows up to be a man?

The rise of rugby in America is even more remarkable when you consider the game exists without government funding or significant gate receipts. The budget for 1990 totalled $382,000 of which sponsorship provided $290,000. According to the latest statistics, there are around 260,000 people involved in the sport, proving that the game has taken root in the American soil from the Pacific to the Atlantic.

These players are spread around 1,311 clubs and the breakdown of that figure will provide an even clearer picture of where the game is being nurtured. The massive country is split into four territories with a total of 413 clubs and the USA Eagles World Cup squad comes from this section. The colleges, which represent the most important area for recruitment, have 392 clubs followed by 101 from the High Schools. There are another 86 clubs formed by military establishments, some based overseas, while 28 are part of professional schools. That leaves 129 clubs catering for the Goldies Oldies (or Masters) age groups and another 162 run by women. The East Coast boasts the strongest section in America with 155 affiliated clubs, with the Metropolitan New York Conference supporting 27. The Mid-West Union has 96 clubs, the Western Rugby Union a total of 65 and the Pacific Coast 74. The

147

The American Eagles clear their lines against England in the 1987 World Cup pool match. England ran out 34–6 winners at Sydney's Concord Oval.

independents, including Alaska, Montana and Hawaii, add 23 to the total.

The USARFU, known as the Eagles, first played an international against Australia in 1976 (a 24–12 defeat) and now is well on the way to its first half century of internationals. The heaviest defeat came at the hands of the Australians who thumped the USA 69–9 in Sydney in July 1990. The best USA win in the tremendously popular cross-border contest with Canada came at Saranac Lake, New York in June 1988 with a 28–16 home victory. The two North American entries in the World Cup have been regular opponents since 1977 and, while Canada has had much the better of the series to date, it's only the occasional encounter that sees a one-sided result. In June 1990 it was close with the Eagles winning 14–12 in Seattle just a week before Canada achieved its unexpected 19–15 World Cup preliminary round victory at the expense of Argentina in Buenos Aires. These three countries had to stage a home and away Americas Zone World Cup tournament to determine pool placings. Canada, by winning twice against the Pumas after a resounding 21–3 success against the Eagles in Toronto, took first place and qualified for the French pool, second placed Argentina travel to Wales leaving the USA to join Italy, cup holders New Zealand and England.

The Canada v USA game in Toronto, in the autumn of 1989, provided yet another example of how one man has left his mark on the series. Mark Wyatt, picked on the wing rather than in his accustomed full-back spot, scored 17 of his team's 21 points from five penalties and a conversion. In 1985, in Vancouver, it was Wyatt 21 and the USA 10.

The Eagles have quickly learned to live with the ever increasing pressure found both on and off the field. They played just twice as a national team in

Barry Williams, the Eagle wing, finds this Netherlands tackler too persistent during the Hong Kong Sevens tournament. Williams is one of the fastest men in the American game.

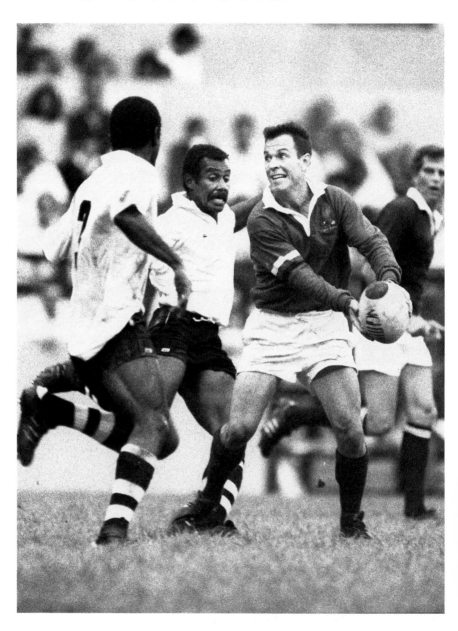

Jim Wilkinson attempts to keep the move alive for the Eagles against Fiji. Despite being a young rugby country this is the USA's second World Cup.

1976 and 1977 but only once in 1978 and 1979. Compare that leisurely pace with the seven games completed in the World Cup year of 1987 followed more recently by four internationals in both 1989 and 1990, among them 23–6 and 13–6 defeats by Argentina. Throughout, the American players, and over 120 have represented their country since 1976, have been gaining in stature and experience. For example, Brian Vizard has won 16 caps dating back to 1986 and with them a considerable reputation as a strong and gifted back-row specialist, one who will likely lead the Eagles to Otley, Gloucester and finally Twickenham where their only previous appearance brought a 37–11 defeat by England back in 1977.

The American players know what lies ahead and will prepare accordingly, pinning their hopes on a squad that will have a high average age (it was 29 at the 1987 World Cup), considerable physical presence up front and an abundance of spirit and pride. Before then they will have faced Japan, Scotland and Canada, in May and June. It's a very full programme, one that will further hone the talents of new names like those of wing Chris Williams and hooker Tony Flay while adding to the stature of such well-established men as lock Kevin Swords, centre Kevin Higgins, wing Gary Hein, the Oxford Blue, and scrum-half Barry Daily. Flay, who has moved ahead of former first choices Pat Johnson and Tom McCormack, and wing Eric Whittaker, were new caps against Japan in 1990 while Higgins and Swords began their Eagle careers together on the side that won 16–15 against Japan in Tokyo in 1985. Since then Higgins, a sturdy and direct runner, has appeared in a record 21 of 22 internationals, one more than US Air force captain Swords, at 6ft 5in and 242 lbs among the biggest men in the American game today and a respected opponent.

For the 1987 World Cup the USA was drawn in the Australian pool while most of the emphasis was on developments in New Zealand. This time they will be right at the heart of the action and determined to make the biggest possible impression against some of the best in the world. The opening assignment against Italy could be well within their scope but they know their challenge to the All Blacks and England will have to be pitched at an extraordinary level if they are to make any impact at all.

Peter McMullan is a Canadian-based rugby writer.

WALES: *The Wales squad;*
Wales finished third in the 1987 World Cup finals.

WALES

by
Robert Cole

When there is an eclipse of the sun people watch in amazement and, sometimes, fear. It's been like that with Welsh rugby of late, as people wonder what has gone wrong with the one-time giants of the game in the northern hemisphere who currently find themselves languishing in the shadow of the rest of the world. The wonderment of outsiders has been matched by the fear of those Welshmen and women who religiously follow every bounce of the ball in their homeland. As the glory days of the seventies creep further and further back into the annals of time, they worry that those days will never be seen again.

But it's just like the Welsh to paint a gloomy picture of their national sport. Just as they love to gloat when things are going well, so they like to agonise over the failings. The Welsh consuming passion for rugby is matched only in intensity by that of New Zealand. The game provides a nation of around 3 million with a common denominator and a national pastime that is taken very seriously. The phrase 'it's only a game' does not enter the equation. It means more, much more than that. Maybe that's why, in the troubled times of late, Welsh rugby has been hogging the front page headlines as well as those on the back. Trauma, drama and intrigue have become the norm throughout the eighties and into the nineties. The outstanding successes of the seventies speak for themselves: three Grand Slams, five Triple Crowns, four of them in succession, and a 27 match unbeaten home run in the Five Nations championship that stretched from 1969 to 1982. These achievements are still fondly recalled by many, although to the modern day players the shadows cast by the giants of that golden age, Gareth Edwards, J.P.R. and J.J. Williams, Barry John, Mervyn and Gerald Davies, Phil Bennett, Allan Martin and Graham

Price are virtually impossible to escape or even momentarily evade.

For the current stars, the seventies have become a burden, a constant reminder of their own inadequacies. There was a sixty year gap between the two greatest eras in Welsh rugby, yet the demand for similar success to that enjoyed only two decades ago remains. While Wales was regarded as one of the top rugby playing nations throughout that time, in 1987 they proved they were right at the top of the tree by finishing third in the inaugural World Cup. That result came only two months after the end of a Five Nations championship series which had seen Wales win only one of their four matches, against England. But when the greatest challenge in world rugby presented itself, Tony Gray's Welsh team pulled itself around and made it through to the semi-finals. Victories over Ireland, in a group match, and England, in the quarter finals, were particularly sweet while Tonga and Canada were also beaten along the way.

Then came a massive set-back. New Zealand have long been major rivals of Wales, and a yardstick for the rest of the rugby playing world. The All Blacks brutally dismissed Wales in the Brisbane semi-final. There were 8 tries, 49 points and some instant retribution for the Welsh second row Huw Richards when he weighed in at a skirmish. The punch from Wayne Shelford that knocked him down was bad enough, but the decision by Australian referee Kerry Fitzgerald to send him off added insult to injury for Richards and Wales. However, that 49–6 defeat was overshadowed by the euphoria which followed the third place play-off triumph over Australia in Rotorua. Paul Thorburn was the hero of the hour with his last ditch touchline conversion of Adrian Hadley's try earning a 22–21 win. The team that had headed down under on a wing and a prayer at least returned with its pride restored.

The turn around in playing fortunes was remarkable. The Triple Crown was secured in the 1987/88 season and once again Wales seemed to be back at the top. In reality that was not the case, as the New Zealanders once again cruelly showed when, as the king pins of Europe, Wales headed south for a suicidal two-test tour. It was an ill-conceived, badly planned tour that showed

The massive frame of Phil Davies, the Welsh No 8, dominates the scene. He is one of the few Welsh forwards who can cause problems on the world stage.

Mike Hall, the Wales and British Lions centre, on the burst with Richie Collins on his shoulder and Kenny Milne (Scotland) attempting the tackle.

up the glaring deficiencies in skill, attitude and application between the Welsh players and the *crème de la crème* of world rugby, and did immeasurable damage to the Welsh game. Two 50 point defeats were hard enough to swallow, but reverses against Waikato, Wellington and North Auckland in provincial matches were even more difficult to stomach.

The tour left Welsh rugby in tatters and caused the Welsh Rugby Union general committee to dispense with the coaching services of Tony Gray and Derek Quinnell. At a time when, more than anything else, a few constants were needed, they became the scapegoats. Their dismissal paved the way for a piece of history when, for the first time, the Union agreed to hand the job over to a non-international player, John Ryan. The former Newport and Cardiff coach was recognised as the best club coach in the business, yet not even he could halt the decline in international results. As he attempted a change

David Evans, the Welsh centre, looks to free Hall with Paul Turner moving up in support against France. Despite their problems, Wales still have dangerous backs.

of style, advocating a more set-piece orientated approach, so the defeats continued. Players came and went as he tried to find a winning combination. After a 28–6 opening triumph over Western Samoa on 12 November 1988, his men lost their next four games, including a disastrous 15–9 home defeat at the hands of the Romanians. Like their bitter experience in New Zealand earlier in the same year, that result hammered home how far Wales had slumped in the world rankings. A 12–9 home win over England at the end of the 1989 Five Nations series, perpetuating the face-saving run over the auld enemy in Cardiff that stretched back to 1963, brought Ryan a brief reprieve. That was to be the second and last win of his nine match reign as coach and in the next three games Wales went down 34–9 to the All Blacks, 29–19 to France and a record 34–6 to England at Twickenham. The latter was Wales' heaviest defeat by England, and their worst showing in the Five Nations championship. Ryan

quickly decided enough was enough, and stepped down to allow a new man to build up to the 1991 World Cup. The WRU handed over control to the highly successful Neath coach Ron Waldron.

To be fair to Gray, Ryan and now Waldron, they have all had to deal with a highly damaging outside force which time after time has wrecked their team building. That influence is rugby league, a professional game that relied heavily on ready-made talent from South Wales during the eighties. If it was nothing really new as a threat to the stability of the international side (a steady procession of Welsh stars had changed codes down the years) the intensity increased greatly at a time when success was elusive. The massive increase in transfer fees had a lot to do with the rush up the M6 and no fewer than sixteen former first-class players, thirteen of them internationals, are currently thriving in the rival code. Is it any wonder that a country robbed of the talents of players like Terry Holmes, David Bishop, Gary Pearce, Adrian Hadley, Jonathan Davies, Stuart Evans, David Young, Paul Moriarty, John Devereux and Jonathan Griffiths is currently struggling? No other nation, not even the Australians or New Zealanders, have suffered so badly. The new opportunities open to amateur players under the revised International Board regulations, allowing them to earn appearance money for certain off-the-field activities and to cash in on their fame in other ways, is bound to provide the WRU with a weapon with which to repel the Northern raiders. But, the feeling is that only success at international level will really be able to stem the flood to a trickle. Waldron is working hard on that aspect, but while he came in on the crest of a wave, having worked small miracles at Neath in conjunction with another former Welsh pack hard man Brian Thomas, he quickly found that success at international level does not come easily.

Ryan ended his reign at Twickenham with four Neath players in his team; Waldron began his with seven against Scotland. Ever since then the Welsh

OPPOSITE: *For many rugby fans this is the best scrum-half pass in the game. Robert Jones, of Wales, whips the ball away with speed and style.*

OVERLEAF: *Arthur Emyr, the Welsh wing, scoring against Scotland. This was Emyr's debut try for his country and he beat Tony Stanger to the line.*

team has relied heavily on the Neath connection, but while they have maintained their amazing run of victories at club level, the same players have found it difficult to transfer that winning formula to the international stage. Their highly fluent game plan has become the role model for the national side. It may be the way forward for Welsh rugby, based as it is on New Zealand principles, and might have earned Neath an unprecedented treble of Merit Table, Western Mail Championship and Schweppes Cup titles in 1990, but it still has its knockers around the club scene. Waldron is working hard to convince players and coaches alike that fitness, togetherness and single mindedness are vital. The revolution is underway but it needs time to spread and develop.

An integral part of the revolution has been the introduction of a structured league system into club rugby. First advocated by Ray Williams twenty years earlier, it eventually became a reality in 1990. The protracted battle that surrounded the introduction provided further evidence of the deep-rooted problems within Welsh rugby. While the WRU governed the game as a whole, the Merit Table group, representing the top eighteen gate-taking clubs, was a self-made governing body within that same organisation. It encompassed the traditional centres of excellence within the game and was the focal point for the best players and the selectors, despite being a very small part of the 205 member clubs of the Union. Its self-interest in perpetuating its position at the top, culminating in a threat to form a breakaway Union, almost thwarted the introduction of the Heineken league system. It took a long time for common sense to prevail, but Welsh rugby is now reaping the benefit at all levels of a four division system that currently involves thirty-eight teams. This figure will rise to fifty in the 1991/92 season and over the next decade the old Merit Table cartel could find itself fragmented by the one-time minnows who for so

OPPOSITE: *Paul Thorburn fights for the high ball with Denis Charvet, of France, at Cardiff. Robert Jones watches the action.*

BELOW: *Paul Thorburn has more time on his hands in the same match and feeds the ball out to Mark Ring, the Welsh centre.*

long have been waiting for their chance to swim in the mainstream. The traditional giants: Cardiff, Swansea, Llanelli, Neath, Newport and Pontypool, are unlikely to come unstuck, although one or two have experienced lean periods. The likes of Penarth, Cross Keys, Ebbw Vale, Tredegar and Glamorgan Wanderers could find themselves overtaken in the new pecking order by Mountain Ash, Dunvant, Cilfynydd, Tenby United and Llanharan before the end of the century. In line with Waldron's thinking for the players, the advent of league rugby has focussed the minds of every club, rather than the elite few, on reaching the highest pinnacles of Welsh rugby.

The down turn in results at international level has only been a part of the general demise of Welsh Rugby Union. When Ray Williams became the first Welsh coaching organiser in the sixties, Wales led the world in off-the-field initiatives. The former Wales and British Lions forward, David Nash, became the first national coach in 1967 and the system created by Williams became the

BELOW: *Mark Ring, the Welsh centre, is left facing four Irish tacklers. Ring has the ability to ignite the Welsh back division.*
OPPOSITE: *Robert Jones, the Welsh scrum-half, clears despite an attempted charge down by Brian Smith, the Irish outside-half. Jones has found himself battling with Chris Bridges for the Welsh No 9 shirt.*

envy of, and ultimately the role model for, the rest of the world. This period coincided with a crop of extraordinarily talented players who came onto the scene at that time and Welsh rugby went from strength to strength. If there was a failure then, and it only became obvious with the passing of time, it was that no long term capital was made out of those golden days. Everyone loved the success that kept on coming, but no one had the foresight to build on it to protect the future.

Money was poured into the rebuilding of the Arms Park, at the expense of grass root development, and when the production line of players began to slow down everyone wondered why. A fundamental change in the education system has compounded these problems. As the grammar schools have been phased out, and tertiary colleges have become the latest invention, so rugby has subsided in the schools. The teachers' strike of the mid-eighties robbed the youngsters of many willing and able rugby coaches and the full impact of that

Wales captain Paul Thorburn is one of rugby's great goal kickers. His boot has kept Wales in games in recent seasons and he will be the main weapon in the World Cup.

loss is only now becoming wholly apparent. Many schools don't run sides and the proliferation of other sports, and opportunities, available to teenagers has meant that rugby misses a lot of its youngsters. But all is not lost for the game in Wales – far from it. That underlying love for rugby is still an inherent part of the Welsh nation and renewed success is only a matter of time. Just how long it will take is difficult to say, although the signs are encouraging. With the bank loans paid on the rebuilding of the now magnificent National Ground, there is money to be invested in the game. This has led to the appointment of seven development officers, responsible for promoting and fostering rugby all over Wales, an overlord for referees, a marketing executive and a technical director. All these positions, and more, came out of the 'Quest for Excellence' guideline document adopted by the Union as it looked into the future. At long last the governing body realised it had to fight its corner in the sporting world.

Heading the combat troops is the latest WRU secretary, Denis Evans. He came to power at the beginning of 1990 following the resignation of David East, the former Chief Constable of South Wales, over the handling of the South African centenary tour plans. The furore that surrounded that trip, which involved ten Welsh players and six committee members, rumbled on for sixteen months and caused no end of embarrassment and headaches. It typified the terrible mess in which Welsh rugby can so easily land itself.

There are encouraging signs of improvement in key areas and the Wales under-21 side has remained unbeaten since its inception in 1987. The Welsh Schools under-18 team was undefeated on their summer tour of New Zealand in 1990. The quality is still there and crowds at Heineken League Premier Division matches are the equivalent of many English League First Division soccer games. The chances of repeating, or improving on, that third place in the inaugural World Cup may not look good, but for those who dare to cast an eye towards 1995 there is more than just a glimmer of light. Slowly, but surely, Welsh rugby is emerging from the shadows and is preparing to come out into the sunlight. The eclipse is ready to clear.

Robert Cole is the Welsh rugby correspondent for the *Sunday Express*.

WESTERN SAMOA: The Western Samoa squad; they were the Pacific qualifying group champions.

WESTERN SAMOA

by
Austin Daniel

Western Samoa forced world rugby to sit up and take notice when they emerged as winners of the World Cup qualifying tournament staged in Japan in May 1990. The Pacific Islanders not only recorded their biggest international victory, 74–7 over South Korea, but accounted for the host country 37–11. Their unbeaten qualifying result sequence was completed by a 12–3 win against Tonga who had taken part in the inaugural 1987 World Cup. Suddenly Australia, Wales and Argentina were joined in their group by a Pacific rugby nation capable of winning on foreign soil.

This state affairs did not come about by accident. Western Samoa appointed key men to take charge of their World Cup qualifying bid in 1989. This plan was mapped out by Alan Grey, chairman of the Western Samoa Rugby Football Union. Lamositele Peter Schuster, brother of former All Black John, had the coaching job and it continued an association with the national team stretching back four years. His coaching has been vital to Western Samoa.

Samoan rugby is unique, utilizing the Islanders' love of dynamic, robust attacking play. Rugby is the national sport of the Island, which boasts a population of 165,000 and is divided into ten sub-unions each containing an average of ten clubs. The enthusiasm borders on ecstacy and according to David Hellaby, the WSRFU secretary, there are 6,000 adult players with the schools providing another 800 to propagate a game that does not, as yet, involve Samoan women.

The WSRFU was formed in 1927 and currently has as its President the Honourable Tupua Tamasese Efi. The Union's first official match came three years before its foundation against Fiji. The WSRFU's birth saw widespread jubilation as the national team scored a famous victory over Fiji in 1927. The

Taufusi Salesa, receiving the pass, is expected to make a big impact on the World Cup. He is the captain and most capped player.

Fijians have always found Samoa difficult opponents and were beaten 26–9 in 1990 in Apia, the Samoan capital. The Samoan players wear blue jerseys, white shirts and blue and white stockings and are noted for long hair and physical toughness. Wales discovered this fact on their Pacific tour. Wales won 32–14 in June, 1986 and defeated Samoa at Cardiff 28–6 in 1988.

The Samoan players have been popular competitors at the Hong Kong Sevens, a tournament that offers the inventive rugby player a world stage. The Western Samoan name has been a regular since the event started in 1976 and few will forget their clash with Australia three years later. The Samoans failed to come to terms with the Wallabies who included the Ella brothers, Mark and Glen, in a final played in mud and rain.

Taufusi Salesa is one player who should make a big impact on the 1991 World Cup. He has played more than twenty times for his country and that makes him Samoa's most capped international. Salesa has also captained Samoa in more games than anyone else and his talents were recognised by South Africa's Dave Stewart. It was Stewart who coached the first multi-racial rugby team to visit South Africa in 1982 and rated Salesa the most naturally

Western Samoa won the Pacific qualifying group in style and their all action rugby will please crowds at the World Cup.

gifted player he had ever seen, by a country of high standards.

Salesa returned to South Africa with the South Pacific Barbarians and many former Springboks felt that the tour party reminded the home players what running rugby could achieve. Besides Salesa in the backs, the Samoans also expect great strides, literally, to be made by Filipo Saena, Timo Tagaloa, Keneti Sio and To'o Mano'o. Up front there should be strong performances in the World Cup from hooker Stan To'omalatai and flanker Danny Kaleopa. Western Samoa rugby has particularly strong links with New Zealand and many players base themselves in the club competitions in that country's main cities. Peter Fatialofa, a 6 ft, 15 stone prop, plays for the Ponsonby club in Auckland and he captains the Western Samoa national team.

Western Samoa took part in the Toulouse centenary tournament held in France in December 1990. A particularly cold spell on their stop over in London affected their handling but it is always beneficial to be forewarned. If Australia, Wales and Argentina fail to prepare properly for the Western Samoa challenge, there could be major upsets in this World Cup group.

Austin Daniel is a freelance rugby writer.

171

ZIMBABWE: *The Zimbabwe squad;*

they were the champions of the African qualifying group.

ZIMBABWE

by
Chris Thau

Zimbabwean rugby received the perfect present for its centenary in 1990 when it secured the African qualifying place for the World Cup. On 5 July 1890 the dry sand-bed of the River Shashi on Zimbabwe's border with Botswana had provided a pioneer column from the Cape with a flat and abrasive surface for that first rugby match. A century later the heirs of that column defeated Morocco, Tunisia and Ivory Coast to claim the right to be Africa's representatives. There had been considerable criticism of the International Board's decision to invite Zimbabwe to be the African group team for the 1987 World Cup in New Zealand and Australia. Now, they had won the place by right.

Rugby has always been hard on its players in Zimbabwe. The vast distances between cities and a sparse population, together with the absence of organised transport, created terrible problems at the turn of the century. A rail link from the south did not reach Harare (or Salisbury as it was then known) until 1901. At that time the Bulawayo players took three weeks to travel 600 miles by coach for a game in the capital.

Even before the inter-provincial matches a representative side, drawn from five clubs, had taken part in the Currie Cup competition in South Africa. In 1898 Rhodesia (as Zimbabwe was then known) returned home from the South having beaten Eastern Province and the Orange Free State and drawn with Transvaal. Rhodesia became part of the South African Rugby Board but lack of funds meant that only six tours to South Africa took place between 1908 and 1946. Not surprisingly, after the earlier successes against the South Africans the quality of Rhodesian rugby dramatically declined. During its first fifty-five years the country played only five international matches, against the Lions in

Zimbabwe found Scotland too strong in the 1987 World Cup and were beaten 60–21. This time they are aiming to put up a better showing.

1910, 1924 and 1938, the All Blacks in 1928 and the Wallabies in 1933. Throughout these years the main achievement of Zimbabwean rugby was its survival.

After the Second World War the well-paid jobs in the copper mining industry in Zambia (at that time part of the Rhodesian Union) and the flourishing tobacco farms attracted many South Africans. Naturally, amongst them there were a large number of top-class rugby players and the fortunes of Rhodesian rugby soon changed. In 1946 Rhodesia beat Western Province and in 1948 Northern Transvaal. The following year they beat the mighty All Blacks by 10–8 in the first test and drew 3–3 in the second and in 1950 the Junior Springboks shared the fate of the New Zealanders. Throughout the 1950s Rhodesia managed to maintain the momentum, with a win against the 1953 Wallabies (16–12) and narrow defeats at the hands of the visiting Lions (16–12) in 1955 and the All Blacks (13–9) in 1960.

Following their success against South Africa in 1950 seven Rhodesians were invited to the Springboks' trials for the 1951 tour to Britain. Three of them made it: Salty du Rand, Ryk van Schoor and Des van Jaarsveldt. The latter, one of the very few born and bred Rhodesians to reach the top, captained the Springboks on his debut against Scotland in 1960. The legendary Jaarsveldt was there to watch his country beat the previously unbeaten Tunisia 24–13 to qualify for the World Cup finals. This remarkable feat has provided the game in Zimbabwe with a timely boost and confirmed the value of the development programme launched by the Zimbabwe Rugby Union in the wake of the 1980 independence.

The independence brought the South African connection to an end. During the 1970s Zimbabwe rugby had enjoyed a decade of unprecedented prosperity and development. Faced with a substantial reduction in the flow of quality rugby players from South Africa after the break-up of the Federation of Rhodesia and Nyasaland in 1963, Rhodesia had developed its own home-bred talent. The unorthodox style of Rhodesian backs made a great impression on the Springbok selections. Rhodesia became one of the most feared provincial sides in the Currie Cup but after 1980, without the support of South Africa, Zimbabwe had to look elsewhere to develop the game and fulfil its international ambitions. Developing the interest of black youngsters was vital for the future of the game and the Zimbabwe Rugby Union launched an ambitious development programme which has begun to pay off.

In 1980 the game was played in about fifty senior and junior schools, mostly, if not exclusively, by white schoolboys. Ten years later the game is played in over 170 schools across the country and approximately 85 per cent of the 10,000 participants are black youngsters. Former Mosely regular Colin Osborne played a significant role as national technical director and rugby is the fastest growing team sport in Zimbabwe. 'A shortage of qualified rugby coaches is the main problem confronting Zimbabwe rugby,' commented the chairman of Mashonaland Union, David Shephard. 'The success of the game in schools has taken us somewhat by surprise.' ZRU Vice-President Sam Waldemar, a resident of Bulawayo (Matabeleland) confirms the predicament of Zimbabwe rugby: 'We have become victims of our own success. Rugby has a very high profile in the country. With soccer in such a mess both at playing and administration levels, rugby is providing the black people with a well-organised and disciplined set up. Four years ago we started to develop the game in the so-called high-density areas, in other words the areas heavily

populated by blacks. We introduced mini-rugby and pushed the game at senior high school level. Bulawayo municipality gave us a turfed ground and we noticed a sudden surge in popularity and interest in the game.'

Centre Richard Tsimba was the first black to represent Zimbabwe in an international and his unconventional talent delighted the knowledgeable New Zealand crowds in the 1987 World Cup. His heirs in the national side are the highly talented wingers Bedford Chibma, Zivanai Dzinomurubi and Haniwell Nguruve, who greatly contributed to the success of their country in the qualifying tournament in Harare playing at No. 8. These three Africans are athletic and skilful and eager to prove themselves. It is up to their New Zealand coach Duncan Rossiter to harness this wealth of talent into a meaningful outfit and try to instil traditional Kiwi rugby values. His main ally in developing a coherent and mistake-free unit is Zimbabwean scrum-half and captain Andy Ferreira who played at full-back in the previous World Cup and is one of the sporting heroes of Zimbabwe. He was one of the initiators of the National Tennis scheme for blacks from townships. A dedicated PE teacher and rugby master, he has won the respect of his players and the support of the fans. Among Zimbabwe forwards hooker Peter Albasini, lock

Anthony Horton and flanker Brendan Dawson have been Ferreira's main trump cards.

Shortage of quality opposition hampers the efforts of the Zimbabwe enthusiasts. However, Zimbabwe, in spite of the obvious imbalance in quality, are prepared to give a good account of themselves against Scotland and Ireland and their moment of glory could come against Japan at Ravenhill in Belfast.

Chris Thau is a freelance rugby writer.

BELOW: *Scotland's Gavin Hastings slices his way through the Zimbabwe defence. He kicked eight conversions to add to the African nation's problems.*

OPPOSITE: *Andy Ferreira (15) played full-back in the 1987 World Cup and he is a sporting hero in Zimbabwe. Ferreira is now playing scrum-half for his country.*

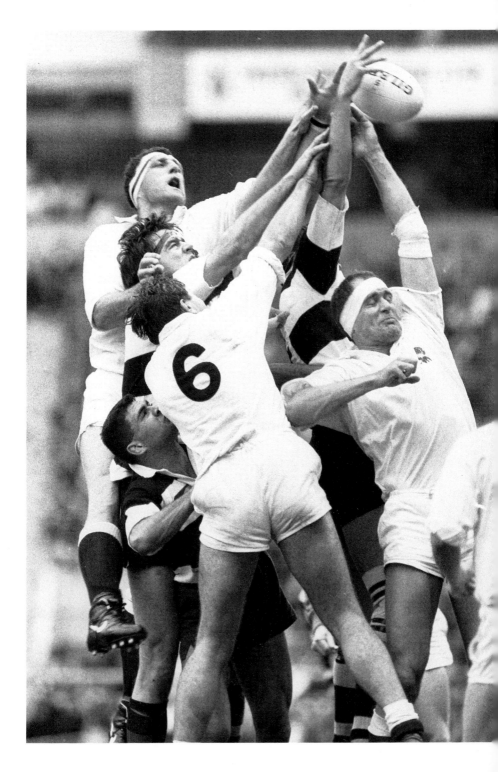

HEAD TO HEAD PREVIEWS OF THE 1991 WORLD CUP GROUP MATCHES

by
John Griffiths

In the following records, major cap matches refer to those for which full members of the International Board have awarded caps, and include all games played during the 1987 World Cup final stages.

These are the only matches considered for drawing up the tables of Cap Match records which follow.

However in the notes an effort is made to record all other representative matches involving the relevant teams, and outstanding performances in these games are also mentioned.

All records are for matches played up to 31 March 1991.

Mike Teague (No 6) adds his height to the England cause as Dooley and Ackford (front) compete with the Barbarian forwards.

GROUP ONE
(Games based in England)

ENGLAND v NEW ZEALAND
Group One Match   3 October at Twickenham   Kick Off 1500

Major Cap Match Records

Played 15, England won 3, New Zealand won 12, Drawn 0.

First Test:	1905	New Zealand	15–0	England	(Crystal Palace)
Recent Tests:	1973	New Zealand	9–0	England	(Twickenham)
	1973	England	16–10	New Zealand	(Auckland)
	1978	New Zealand	16–6	England	(Twickenham)
	1979	New Zealand	10–9	England	(Twickenham)
	1983	England	15–9	New Zealand	(Twickenham)
	1985	New Zealand	18–13	England	(Christchurch)
	1985	New Zealand	42–15	England	(Wellington)

England Cap Match Records

Highest score	16 in 1973
Biggest winning margin	13 in 1936
Most tries	3 in 1936
	3 in 1973
Most points by a player	11 by W H Hare in 1983
Most tries by a player	2 by A Obolensky in 1936
	2 by R H Lloyd in 1967
Most conversions by a player	2 by P A Rossborough in 1973
	2 by S Barnes in 1985
Most penalties by a player	3 by W H Hare in 1979
	3 by W H Hare in 1983

New Zealand Cap Match Records

Highest score	42 in 1985
Biggest winning margin	27 in 1985
Most tries	6 in 1985
Most points by a player	18 by K J Crowley in 1985
Most tries by a player	4 by D McGregor in 1905

Most conversions by a player   4 by W F McCormick in 1967

Most penalties by a player   6 by K J Crowley in 1985

Memorabilia

☐ Of the nine matches between the sides at Twickenham, England have won two and New Zealand seven. During the first match at the ground, in 1925, Cyril Brownlie was sent off by Welsh referee Albert Freethy.

☐ The try-count is more than 2:1 in New Zealand's favour. The All Blacks have scored 35 to England's 17 in the series.

☐ The only full-back who has scored a try in the games was Don Clarke of New Zealand at Auckland in 1963.

☐ The New Zealander scored with four different actions in that match: a try, conversions, a penalty and a dropped goal. At Christchurch in 1963 Clarke kicked the only goal from a mark scored in matches between the teams.

☐ Englishman Jamie Salmon holds the unique distinction of playing tests for both sides. He won three caps for New Zealand in 1981 and 12 for England between 1985–87, including two against New Zealand in 1985.

☐ There have been two other representative matches involving England and New Zealand teams:

1889   England   7–0   NZ Maoris   (Blackheath)

1945   NZ Kiwis   18–3   England XV   (Twickenham)

☐ England awarded caps for the 1889 game, but neither side gave caps for the Victory international in 1945, which was the first representative match played at Twickenham after World War Two.

ITALY v UNITED STATES

Group One Match   5 October at Otley   Kick Off 1300

Major Cap Match Records

NONE

Memorabilia

☐ There has been no previous meeting of the senior teams at representative level.

☐ Italy toured North America in 1983 (playing two tests against Canada) but did not meet the Eagles in a test.

NEW ZEALAND v UNITED STATES

Group One Match   8 October at Gloucester   Kick Off 1300

Major Cap Match Records

Played 1, New Zealand won 1, United States won 0, Drawn 0.

First Test: 1913 New Zealand   51–3   United States   (Berkeley)

New Zealand Cap Match Records

Highest score	51 in 1913
Biggest winning margin	48 in 1913
Most tries	13 in 1913
Most points by a player	9 by R W Roberts in 1913
Most tries by a player	3 by R W Roberts in 1913
Most conversions by a player	4 by J B Graham in 1913
Most penalties by a player	None

United States Cap Match Records

Highest score	3 in 1913
Biggest winning margin	No win
Most tries	None
Most points by a player	3 by S B Pert in 1913
Most tries by a player	None
Most conversions by a player	None
Most penalties by a player	1 by S B Pert in 1913

Memorabilia

☐ The All Blacks sent a tour party to North America in October and November 1913 and gave the test match full international status.

☐ The American side in 1913 was drawn entirely from Californian clubs. Their centre Danny Carroll had previously played for Australia and won gold medals at the Olympics of 1908 (for Australia) and 1920 (for the United States).

☐ New Zealand's total and winning margin in 1913 stood as national records until the 1987 World Cup.

☐ There has been one other representative match between the sides:

1980 New Zealand   53–6   United States   (San Diego)

☐ New Zealand did not award caps for this match which was played by Graham Mourie's side en route to Wales. The game was played under floodlights and 10000 saw S W Gray lead the Eagles.

☐ The All Blacks scored eight tries, including a hat-trick by Fred Woodman. Full-back Brett Codlin's haul of 21 points comprised six conversions and three penalties. Scrum-half Dick Cooke scored the American points with two penalty goals.

Grant Fox, the New Zealand scoring machine, fires another kick goalwards. He made a big impact on the 1987 tournament and finished top scorer.

ENGLAND v ITALY

Group One Match   8 October at Twickenham   Kick Off 1500

Major Cap Match Records

NONE

Memorabilia

☐ The first match played in England between Italian and English teams was in 1951 when Rugby Roma beat London 11–3.

☐ Four years later an Italian representative side played for the first time at Twickenham, losing 11–22 against London Counties.

☐ There have been seven representative matches but England have never previously awarded caps for their games against Italy:

1975	England U-23	29–13	Italy	(Gosforth)
1979	Italy	6–6	England U-23	(Brescia)
1982	Italy	12–7	England U-23	(Padua)
1985	England B	21–9	Italy	(Twickenham)
1986	Italy	15–15	England B	(Rome)
1990	England XV	33–15	Italy XV	(Rovigo)

☐ Stefano Bettarello scored 12 points for Italy in the 1982 win at Padua.

☐ Three Italian players have kicked three penalties in a game: Ennio Ponzi (1975), Stefano Bettarello (1986) and Luigi Troiani (1990).

☐ Bettarello, who played four times for Italy against English representative sides, scored 34 points altogether (eight penalties, two conversions and two dropped goals). The four Italian tries scored up to 1991 were by wing threequarters.

☐ England won at Waterloo, March 1991, in the most recent 'B' match between the countries.

ENGLAND v UNITED STATES

Group One Match   11 October at Twickenham   Kick Off 1500

Major Cap Match Records

Played 1, England won 1, United States won 0, Drawn 0.

First Test: 1987 England   34–6   United States   (Sydney)

England Cap Match Records

Highest score	34 in 1987
Biggest winning margin	28 in 1987
Most tries	4 in 1987
Most points by a player	18 by J M Webb in 1987
Most tries by a player	2 by P J Winterbottom in 1987
Most conversions by a player	3 by J M Webb in 1987
Most penalties by a player	4 by J M Webb in 1987

United States Cap Match Records

Highest score	6 in 1987
Biggest winning margin	No win
Most tries	1 in 1987
Most points by a player	4 by M Purcell in 1987
Most tries by a player	1 by M Purcell in 1987
Most conversions by a player	1 by R Nelson in 1987
Most penalties by a player	None

Memorabilia

☐ The only previous meeting for which England awarded caps was in the 1987 World Cup when the two sides were grouped in the Australian-based Pool One.

Scrum-half Pietrosanti chips ahead during the match with an England XV in Rovigo in 1990.

185

☐ Ed Burlingham (for United States) and Mike Harrison (for England) were the captains.

☐ There have been two other representative matches between the countries:

| 1977 | England XV | 37–11 | United States | (Twickenham) |
| 1982 | England XV | 59–0 | United States | (Hartford) |

☐ Craig Sweeney, who died tragically shortly after returning from England in 1977, led the Eagles at Twickenham that year. Derek Wyatt scored four tries for England in that game and Dusty Hare kicked 13 points. Bill Beaumont was the England XV's captain.

☐ Hare was England's chief scorer with 20 points in 1982. He converted seven of England's nine tries and kicked two penalties. Steve Smith captained England. S Niebauer was the American captain.

NEW ZEALAND v ITALY

Group One Match   13 October at Leicester   Kick Off 1500

Major Cap Match Records

Played 1, New Zealand won 1, Italy won 0, Drawn 0.

| First Test: | 1987 New Zealand | 70–6 | Italy | (Auckland) |

New Zealand Cap Match Records

Highest score	70 in 1987
Biggest winning margin	64 in 1987
Most tries	12 in 1987
Most points by a player	22 by G J Fox in 1987
Most tries by a player	2 by D E Kirk in 1987
	2 by J J Kirwan in 1987
	2 by C I Green in 1987
Most conversions by a player	8 by G J Fox in 1987
Most penalties by a player	2 by G J Fox in 1987

Italy Cap Match Records

Highest score	6 in 1987
Biggest winning margin	No win
Most tries	None
Most points by a player	6 by O Collodo in 1987
Most tries by a player	None
Most conversions by a player	None
Most penalties by a player	1 by O Collodo in 1987

Memorabilia

☐ The only previous meeting for which New Zealand awarded caps was the 1987 World Cup curtain-raiser when the sides were grouped in Pool Three. New Zealand's winning margin remains a world record for a major test.

☐ Oscar Collodo (Italy) dropped the only goal of that match.

☐ There have been two other representative matches:

1979	New Zealand XV	18–12	Italy	(Rovigo)
1980	NZ Juniors	30–13	Italy	(Auckland)

☐ Only the Italian's awarded caps for these matches. Stefano Bettarello was their leading points-scorer in the games, kicking 11 points.

☐ In the 1979 match the All Blacks, returning from a tour of Scotland and England, were forced to work hard for their narrow win. Allan Hewson kicked 7 of their points before retiring injured after half-time.

☐ Two Italian players, Fulvio Lorigiola and Giuseppe Artuso played in all three Italian sides against the teams of 1979, 1980 and 1987.

Bonomi passes to Barba as Italy launch an attack. Their forwards will struggle against the All Blacks at Leicester.

GROUP TWO
(Games based in Scotland/Ireland)

Finlay Calder in action for Scotland against Japan. Calder was a massive influence on Scottish rugby until his retirement in 1990.

SCOTLAND v JAPAN
Group Two Match   5 October at Murrayfield   Kick Off 1500

Major Cap Match Records

NONE

Memorabilia

☐ Before the sides first met in 1976 two former Scottish caps, Alastair Biggar and Ian Smith played in an international against Japan. In 1972 they were members of the Hong Kong team (coached by current WRU secretary Denis Evans) that lost 0–16 to Japan in the All-Asia tournament.

☐ There have been four representative matches but Scotland have never previously awarded caps for their games with Japan:

1976	Scotland XV	34–9	Japan	(Murrayfield)
1977	Scotland XV	74–9	Japan	(Tokyo)
1986	Scotland XV	33–18	Japan	(Murrayfield)
1989	Japan	28–24	Scotland XV	(Tokyo)

☐ Japan's victory against Scotland in 1989 was their first in any representative match against British or Irish national fifteens. The side scored five tries during their victory in a match controlled by Les Peard of Wales.

☐ Colin Mair holds the record for most points scored in a match. He kicked 30 points, made up of nine conversions and four penalties in 1977. Scotland scored eleven tries in that match.

☐ Two Scotsmen have scored four tries in a match. Bill Gammell crossed four times in 1977 and Iwan Tukalo equalled the record in 1986. Gammell also scored twice in 1976 and holds the overall try-scoring record for the series.

☐ Greig Oliver set a record in Scotland's 1989 defeat, kicking five penalties in the match.

☐ Eiji Kutsuki was the only Japanese to score two tries in the series. His scores came in the 1986 and 1989 matches.

☐ Toshitugu Yamamoto holds the Japanese record for most points in a match. His 12 points in the 1989 test comprised a try, conversion and two penalty goals.

☐ The only dropped goals in the series were scored by Katsuhiro Matsuo (for Japan in 1986) and Douglas Wyllie (for Scotland in 1989).

IRELAND v ZIMBABWE

Group Two Match   6 October at Dublin   Kick Off 1500

Major Cap Match Records

NONE

Memorabilia

☐ There has been one representative match but Ireland did not award caps for the previous game with Rhodesia:

1961	Ireland XV	24–0	Rhodesia	(Salisbury)

☐ The match was the last game of Ireland's first tour to Southern Africa.

☐ Tony O'Reilly led the Irish side in the absence of tour skipper Ronnie Dawson. Ireland won comfortably with Tom Kiernan contributing 12 points from three conversions and two penalties. Des van Jaarsveldt captained Rhodesia.

☐ Fly half Gerry Tormey and wing Niall Brophy both scored two tries for Ireland.

☐ The brothers Ian and Jimmy Dick played together in the Irish pack. Jimmy Dick, who broke a rib during the match, later returned to Rhodesia and hooked for the Old Hararians club.

☐ James Gardiner of Belfast played thirteen times as a scrum-half and threequarter for Ireland before emigrating to Rhodesia during the 1920s to become a cattle rancher. He played for his adopted country in 1928 against the All Blacks.

☐ Another former Irish international, Bill Cunningham, was half back for Rhodesia in the same team as Gardiner in 1928. In 1924, after he had emigrated to Southern Africa, Cunningham was drafted into the Lions team for a test match when the tourists were severely affected by injuries. Cunningham won eight caps for Ireland between 1920–23.

SCOTLAND v ZIMBABAWE

Group Two Match   9 October at Murrayfield   Kick Off 1500

Major Cap Match Records

Played 1, Scotland won 1, Zimbabwe won 0, Drawn 0.

First Test: 1987   Scotland   60–21   Zimbabwe   (Wellington)

Scotland Cap Match Records

Highest score	60 in 1987
Biggest winning margin	39 in 1987
Most tries	11 in 1987
Most points by a player	20 by A G Hastings in 1987
Most tries by a player	2 by A V Tait in 1987
	2 by M D F Duncan in 1987
	2 by I Tukalo in 1987
	2 by I A M Paxton in 1987
Most conversions by a player	8 by A G Hastings in 1987
Most penalties by a player	None

Zimbabwe Cap Match Records

Highest score	21 in 1987
Biggest winning margin	No win
Most tries	1 in 1987

Most points by a player	17 by M Grobler in 1987
Most tries by a player	1 by D Buitendag in 1987
Most conversions by a player	1 by M Grobler in 1987
Most penalties by a player	5 by M Grobler in 1987

Memorabilia

☐ The previous cap match between the sides was in Pool Four during the last World Cup in New Zealand. Colin Deans and Malcolm Jellicoe were the rival captains.

☐ There have been two other representative matches between the teams. Scotland did not award caps for the games played during a five-match tour of Zimbabwe:

1988	Scotland XV	31–10	Zimbabwe	(Bulawayo)
1988	Scotland XV	34–7	Zimbabwe	(Harare)

☐ Full back Peter Dods, the captain, scored 30 points in the two matches and his haul of 19 points in the second test included three penalties.

Scotland's Keith Robertson gets the ball away despite the close attentions of two Zimbabwe players in their 1987 meeting.

□ Andy Ferreira captained Zimbabwe in the first test but Malcolm Jellicoe took over for the second test.

□ Greig Oliver scored the only hat-trick of the series during the first test at Bulawayo in 1988.

□ Marthinus Grobler kicked three penalties in the 1988 tests for Zimbabwe. Ralph Kuhn and Julian Kamba scored Zimbabwe's tries.

□ The only dropped goal kicked in matches between the nations was by Craig Chalmers at Harare in 1988.

□ Matt Duncan, Douglas Wyllie, Greig Oliver (for Scotland) and Marthinus Grobler and Dirk Buitendag (for Zimbabwe) were the only players to feature in the 1987 and 1988 games.

□ The only Rhodesian selected to captain South Africa in a test was Des van Jaarsveldt, in 1960. His appointment was for a test against Scotland that year. ('Salty' du Rand, a former Rhodesian player, led the Springboks in 1956 when he was a Northern Transvaal forward.)

IRELAND v JAPAN

Group Two Match   9 October at Dublin   Kick Off 1500

Major Cap Match Records

NONE

Memorabilia

□ There have been two representative matches but Ireland have never previously awarded caps for their games with Japan:

| 1985 | Ireland XV | 48–13 | Japan | (Osaka) |
| 1985 | Ireland XV | 33–15 | Japan | (Tokyo) |

□ Ciaran Fitzgerald led the Irish tourists in the two tests. Ireland scored eight tries in the first match and four in the second. Japan, who were skippered by Koji Horaguchi, scored two tries in both games.

□ The record for most points in a match was set by Michael Kiernan at Tokyo. He scored 25 points with two tries, four conversions and three penalties, having scored 20 points in the game at Osaka.

□ Trevor Ringland scored the only hat-trick of tries in the series during the test at Osaka.

□ The points record for Japan was set by Hideo Kobayashi at Tokyo. He scored two conversions and a penalty goal.

□ Derek Bevan of Wales refereed both of the tests.

SCOTLAND v IRELAND

Group Two Match   12 October at Murrayfield   Kick Off 1330

Major Cap Match Records

Played 102, Scotland won 52, Ireland won 45, Drawn 4, Abandoned 1.

First Test:	1877† Scotland		4G 2DG 2T–0	Ireland	(Belfast)

Recent Tests:	1985	Ireland	18–15	Scotland	(Murrayfield)
	1986	Scotland	10–9	Ireland	(Dublin)
	1987	Scotland	16–12	Ireland	(Murrayfield)
	1988	Ireland	22–18	Scotland	(Dublin)
	1989	Scotland	37–21	Ireland	(Murrayfield)
	1990	Scotland	13–10	Ireland	(Dublin)
	1991	Scotland	28–25	Ireland	(Murrayfield)

(† before scoring by points was introduced)

Scotland Cap Match Records

Highest score	37 in 1989
Biggest winning margin	23 in 1984
Most tries	7 in 1913
Most points by a player	17 by P W Dods in 1989
Most tries by a player	4 by W A Stewart in 1913
Most conversions by a player	4 by M Cross in 1877
	4 by F H Turner in 1913
	4 by P W Dods in 1989
Most penalties by a player	4 by A R Irvine in 1976
	4 by P W Dods in 1985

Ireland Cap Match Records

Highest score	26 in 1953
Biggest winning margin	21 in 1950
Most tries	6 in 1953
Most points by a player	21 by S O Campbell in 1982
Most tries by a player	3 by E O'D Davy in 1930
	3 by S J Byrne in 1953
Most conversions by a player	4 by P F Murray in 1932
	4 by R J Gregg in 1953
Most penalties by a player	6 by S O Campbell in 1982

Memorabilia

☐ Of the 30 previous meetings at Murrayfield, Scotland have won 12, Ireland 17 and the match in 1979 was drawn – the only tie in the series since 1900.

☐ Four players (all Scots) have dropped two goals in a match. R C Mackenzie (1877), Ninian Finlay (1880), Douglas Morgan (1973) and John Rutherford (1987) set Scotland on the road to victories with their goals.

☐ The goal from a mark was a scoring action which became obsolete in 1977–78 when the Laws of the game changed. Mike Sayers kicked the last goal in the series to help Ireland defeat Scotland in 1939.

☐ The only penalty try in the series was awarded to Scotland by Fred Howard of England in 1984. Scotland won the match and took the Triple Crown.

☐ Tom Kiernan was the first full-back to score a try in the games, in 1973, on his final appearance for Ireland. Andy Irvine (1979), Peter Dods (1984), Fergus Dunlea (1989) and Gavin Hastings (1991) were the only full-backs to repeat the feat.

☐ Two backs, Peter Dods and Keith Robertson, played for Scotland in their highest score and biggest winning points margin against Ireland in 1989 and 1984.

☐ The aggregate of 58 points in the 1989 match created a record for the series.

☐ Derek White (last year) was the first forward in the series to score two tries in a match since Ken Ross did so for Scotland in 1961 at Murrayfield.

☐ There has been one other representative match between the countries:

1946   Scotland XV   9–0   Ireland XV   (Murrayfield)

☐ This game was a Victory international and neither side awarded caps for the game.

ZIMBABWE v JAPAN

Group Two Match   14 October at Belfast   Kick Off 1500

Major Cap Match Records

NONE

Memorabilia

☐ There has been no previous meeting of the teams at representative level.

GROUP THREE
(Games based in Wales)

AUSTRALIA v ARGENTINA
Group Three Match   4 October at Llanelli   Kick Off 1500

Major Cap Match Records

Played 8, Australia won 4, Argentina won 3, Drawn 1.

First Test:	1979	Argentina	24–13	Australia	(Buenos Aires)
Other Tests:	1979	Australia	17–12	Argentina	(Buenos Aires)
	1983	Argentina	18–3	Australia	(Brisbane)
	1983	Australia	29–13	Argentina	(Sydney)
	1986	Australia	39–19	Argentina	(Brisbane)
	1986	Australia	26–0	Argentina	(Sydney)
	1987	Argentina	19–19	Australia	(Buenos Aires)
	1987	Argentina	27–19	Australia	(Buenos Aires)

Australia Cap Match Records

Highest score	39 in 1986
Biggest winning margin	26 in 1986
Most tries	5 in 1983
Most points by a player	23 by M P Lynagh in 1986
Most tries by a player	2 by B J Moon in 1979
	2 by B J Moon in 1983
	2 by B Papworth in 1986
	2 by D I Campese in 1986
	2 by I M Williams in 1987
Most conversions by a player	4 by M P Lynagh in 1986
Most penalties by a player	5 by M P Lynagh in 1986

Argentina Cap Match Records

Highest score	27 in 1987
Biggest winning margin	15 in 1983
Most tries	3 in 1986
Most points by a player	23 by H Porta in 1987
Most tries by a player	2 by R M Madero in 1979

Most conversions by a player	2 by H Porta in 1979
	2 by H Porta in 1983
Most penalties by a player	5 by H Porta in 1987

Memorabilia

☐ The record for most dropped goals in a test was set by Hugo Porta in 1979 during the first meeting of the sides. He kicked three.

☐ Porta, who has only missed one of the previous eight tests between the sides, holds the overall points record for the series. He scored 86 points, made up of seven conversions, nine dropped goals and fifteen penalties.

☐ Michael Lynagh, Australia's leading points-scorer in the series, obtained his 59 points in the 1986 and 1987 matches. His points comprised eight conversions, thirteen penalties and a try scored in the first test in 1987 when he was playing as a centre.

☐ Brendan Moon and David Campese with four apiece share the record of most tries in the series. Campese's tries were scored from the full-back position.

☐ Clive Norling was the referee in 1983 and awarded the only penalty try recorded in the games during the second test at Sydney.

Western Samoa's Keneti Sio is tackled by Nigel Davies, of Wales, in 1988. Wales won this match 28–6 and hold a 2–0 advantage over the Islanders.

☐ The popular prop-forward Enrique Rodriguez ('Topol') appeared in all eight of the previous tests. He played for Argentina in the 1979 and 1983 games, emigrated to Australia, and played against his native country in 1986 and 1987.

☐ The only other player who featured in every test of the series was Rafael Madero. At Brisbane in 1986 he came on as a replacement when Porta was injured and captained the Pumas in the following test in Porta's continued absence. In the other tests against Australia Hugo Porta was Argentina's captain.

WALES v WESTERN SAMOA

Group Three Match   6 October at Cardiff   Kick Off 1300

Major Cap Match Records

Played 2, Wales won 2, Western Samoa won 0, Drawn 0.

First Test: 1986 Wales   32–14 Western Samoa (Apia)

Other Test: 1988 Wales   28–6   Western Samoa (Cardiff)

Wales Cap Match Records

Highest score	32 in 1986
Biggest winning margin	22 in 1988
Most tries	5 in 1988
Most points by a player	13 by M Dacey in 1986
Most tries by a player	2 by N G Davies in 1988
Most conversions by a player	4 by P H Thorburn in 1988
Most penalties by a player	3 by M Dacey in 1986

Western Samoa Cap Match Records

Highest score	14 in 1986
Biggest winning margin	No win
Most tries	2 in 1986
Most points by a player	6 by A Aiolupo in 1986
Most tries by a player	1 by three players
Most conversions by a player	1 by A Aiolupo in 1988
Most penalties by a player	2 by A Aiolupo in 1986

Memorabilia

☐ Wales is the only full member of the International Board that has played a major cap match in

Western Samoa. Their match in 1986, watched by a crowd of 25,000, was the final game of a short tour of the South Pacific.

☐ Richard Moriarty led Wales in the 1986 match after taking over from tour captain David Pickering who was injured playing against Fiji. Moriarty played with his brother Paul in the tour tests. They were the first brothers to appear together in the Welsh pack since 1937.

☐ The only dropped goal scored in the series was by Jonathan Davies in 1986. He captained Wales at Cardiff in the 1988 match.

☐ Davies, Bleddyn Bowen, Robert Jones, Bob Norster and Phil Davies played in both of the previous matches.

☐ Lolani Koko, Stan Toomalati and Aneterea Aiolupo played for Western Samoa in both tests. Koko was the captain of the 1988 team.

☐ Michael Jones, a star of the 1987 New Zealand World Cup squad, played for Western Samoa as a back-row forward in the 1986 test.

WALES v ARGENTINA
Group Three Match   9 October at Cardiff   Kick Off 2000

Major Cap Match Records

NONE

Memorabilia

☐ There have been four representative matches but Wales have never previously awarded caps for their games against Argentina:

1968	Argentina	9–5	Wales XV	(Buenos Aires)
1968	Argentina	9–9	Wales XV	(Buenos Aires)
1976	Wales XV	20–19	Argentina	(Cardiff)
1978	Argentina	17–14	Wales B	(Llanelli)

☐ Only the Argentinians awarded caps for these matches.

☐ In 1968 Wales made a short tour of Argentina under the captaincy of John Dawes who was the only previously-capped back in the party. Phil Bennett and J P R Williams were among the young Welsh players blooded on this tour.

☐ In the first test in 1968 John Dawes converted a try by scrum-half Glen Turner. Swansea wing, Stuart Ferguson, scored Wales's points in the drawn second test. Seaton, the Argentinian full-back, scored 12 of his side's 18 test points in the two games with four penalties.

☐ Phil Bennett was the Welsh match-winner in 1976. After trailing 6–17 the Pumas made a strong rally and led the Welsh XV 19–17 near no side. Then Bennett kicked a penalty from 40 metres after J P R Williams had been late-tackled.

☐ Gonzalo Beccar Varela kicked two penalties and scored a try; Hugo Porta converted a try by Jorge Gauweloose and kicked a penalty for the Pumas. Adolfo Etchegaray led the side from scrum-half.

☐ Terry Cobner captained the Welsh XV in 1976. Gareth Edwards and Gerald Davies scored tries and altogether Phil Bennett kicked four penalties.

☐ Porta returned to Wales in 1978 as captain. His penalty and dropped goal helped his team to a 3-point win against a Wales B team that included Elgan Rees, Peter Morgan, Richard Moriarty and Paul Ringer.

☐ Welsh international rugby's first connection with Argentina was in 1912–13 when a Patagonian named Juan Morgan, who had been educated at Llandovery College and played for Llanelli, won caps for Wales against the South Africans and England.

AUSTRALIA v WESTERN SAMOA
Group Three Match   9 October at Pontypool   Kick Off 1300

Major Cap Match Records

NONE

Memorabilia

☐ There has been no previous meeting of the senior teams at representative level.

WALES v AUSTRALIA
Group Three Match   12 October at Cardiff   Kick Off 1515

Major Cap Match Records

Played 13, Wales won 8, Australia won 5, Drawn 0.†

(† between this book going to press and the World Cup, Wales were due to play Australia in July)

First Test:	1908	Wales	9–6	Australia	(Cardiff)
Recent Tests:	1973	Wales	24–0	Australia	(Cardiff)
	1975	Wales	28–3	Australia	(Cardiff)
	1978	Australia	18–8	Wales	(Brisbane)

1978	Australia	19–17	Wales	(Sydney)
1981	Wales	18–13	Australia	(Cardiff)
1984	Australia	28–9	Wales	(Cardiff)
1987	Wales	22–21	Australia	(Rotorua)

Wales Cap Match Records

Highest score	28 in 1975
Biggest winning margin	25 in 1975
Most tries	4 in 1975
Most points by a player	12 by P Bennett in 1973
	12 by J J Williams in 1975
Most tries by a player	3 by J J Williams in 1975
Most conversions by a player	2 by K S Jarrett in 1969
	2 by S P Fenwick in 1975
	2 by P H Thorburn in 1987
Most penalties by a player	4 by P Bennett in 1973

Australia Cap Match Records

Highest score	28 in 1984
Biggest winning margin	19 in 1984
Most tries	4 in 1927
	4 in 1984

Paul Thorburn on the attack against Australia in the World Cup play-off match in 1987 which saw Wales claim third place in the tournament.

Most points by a player	14 by P E McLean in 1978
Most tries by a player	2 by A C Wallace in 1927
Most conversions by a player	3 by T Lawton in 1927
	3 by R G Gould in 1984
Most penalties by a player	4 by P E McLean in 1978

Memorabilia

☐ Of the nine previous matches at Cardiff, Wales have won six and Australia three.

☐ The 1927 match is now regarded as a full Australian test match, the Australian Rugby Union retrospectively granting the New South Wales (Waratahs) side full Aussie test status in 1986.

☐ Tom Lawton, the outstanding Australian fly-half of the 1920s and scorer of three conversions in the 1927 game against Wales, was the grandfather of hooker Tom Lawton who played against Wales in 1984 (scoring a try) and 1987 (in the World Cup third/fourth place Play Off match).

☐ Gerald Davies, Wales's most-capped threequarter, began and finished his career with matches against Australia (1966–78). Altogether he played five times against the Wallabies and created a record for the series, scoring four tries.

☐ The only tries scored by full-backs in the series were by Australians. Jim Lenehan crossed in the left corner at the Taff End at Cardiff in 1966 and his successor, Arthur McGill scored at Sydney in 1969.

☐ There have been eight dropped goals in the series. Carwyn James was the first player to register such a score in the games, in 1958.

☐ Gareth Davies, who was a pupil at Gwendraeth Grammar School like Carwyn James, was the only player who dropped two goals in the series. He scored in the 1978 and 1981 games.

☐ Dai Morris, Welsh flanker in the 1969 and 1973 matches, was the only forward to score two tries in the series. Brothers Richard and Paul Moriarty hold the unusual distinction of both scoring tries against Australia.

ARGENTINA v WESTERN SAMOA
Group Three Match   13 October at Pontypridd   Kick Off 1300

Major Cap Match Records
NONE

Memorabilia

☐ There has been no previous meeting of the sides at representative level.

GROUP FOUR
(Games based in France)

FRANCE v ROMANIA

Group Four Match   4 October at Béziers   Kick Off 2000

Major Cap Match Records

Played 35, France won 25, Romania won 8, Drawn 2.†

(† between this book going to press and the World Cup, France were due to play Romania in June)

First Test:	1924	France	59–3	Romania	(Paris)
Recent Tests:	1984	France	18–3	Romania	(Bucharest)
	1986	France	25–13	Romania	(Lille)
	1986	France	20–3	Romania	(Bucharest)
	1987	France	55–12	Romania	(Wellington)
	1987	France	49–3	Romania	(Agen)
	1988	France	16–12	Romania	(Bucharest)
	1990	Romania	12–6	France	(Auch)

France Cap Match Records

Highest score	59 in 1924
Biggest winning margin	56 in 1924
Most tries	13 in 1924
Most points by a player	25 by P Bérot in 1987
Most tries by a player	4 by A Jauréguy in 1924
Most conversions by a player	8 by G Laporte in 1987
Most penalties by a player	4 by M Vannier in 1957

Romania Cap Match Records

Highest score	15 on several occasions
Biggest winning margin	15 in 1980
Most tries	3 in 1976
Most points by a player	15 by V Irimescu in 1968
Most tries by a player	1 by several
Most conversions by a player	1 by several

Eric Champ on the rampage for France as they brushed Romania aside in the first World Cup. France ran out 55–12 winners in Wellington.

Most penalties by a player	4 by V Irimescu in 1968
	4 by R Bezuscu in 1987

Memorabilia

☐ The first match for which France awarded caps was during the 1924 Olympic Games. The French won so easily, apparently, that details of the final score vary. The official total was given as 59–3, but some newspaper accounts of the game credit Louis Béguet with an eighth conversion during the match, making the unofficial result 61–3.

☐ Last year's 12–6 win was Romania's first ever on French soil. Fly-half Gelu Ignat kicked all of his side's points.

☐ The only previous meeting of the teams at Béziers was in 1971 when France, led by Benoit

Dauga, won 31–12. It was in that match that Irimescu, the Romanian centre, kicked the only goal from a mark recorded in the series.

☐ Serge Blanco made most appearances for France against Romania, playing ten times between 1980–90. Gheorge Dumitru was Romania's most experienced player: he made 14 appearances between 1973–87.

☐ The largest attendance in the series was 95,000 at Bucharest in 1957. France struggled to win that game 18–15, full-back Michel Vannier contributing four penalties and a dropped goal.

☐ The only player in the series who has dropped two goals in a game was A Penciu in 1960.

☐ There have been four other representative matches between the countries:

1919	France XV	48–5	Romania	(Paris)
1936	France XV	25–3	Romania	(Berlin)
1937	France XV	27–11	Romania	(Paris)
1977	France XV	9–6	Romania	(Paris)

☐ France did not award caps for these matches.

FIJI v CANADA
Group Four Match   5 October at Bayonne   Kick Off 2000

Major Cap Match Records

NONE

Memorabilia

☐ The sides have never previously met in the World Cup but there has been one other representative match:

1970	Fiji	35–17	Canada	(Burnaby)

☐ The match took place on 28 November when the Fijian side, led by Sela Toga, were returning from an autumn tour of Britain. R.N. MacDonald captained Canada.

☐ Spence McTavish, Canada's longest-serving internationalist, won the first of his 22 caps in the 1970 game and scored a try. He retired after the 1987 World Cup. Ro Hindson matched his career record (17 test seasons: 1973–90).

☐ Barry Burnham kicked 11 of Canada's points with three penalties and a conversion.

☐ The Fijians scored nine tries, Ravuama Latilevu and Vuniani Varo both crossing twice. Isimeli Batibasaga converted four.

FRANCE v FIJI

Group Four Match   8 October at Grenoble   Kick Off 2000

Major Cap Match Records

Played 2, France won 2, Fiji won 0, Drawn 0.

First Test:	1964	France	21–3	Fiji	(Paris)
Other Test:	1987	France	31–16	Fiji	(Auckland)

France Cap Match Records

Highest score	31 in 1987
Biggest winning margin	18 in 1964
Most tries	5 in 1964
Most points by a player	15 by G Laporte in 1987
Most tries by a player	2 by C Darrouy in 1964
	2 by J-P Capdouze in 1964
	2 by L Rodriguez in 1987
Most conversions by a player	3 by P Dedieu in 1964
	3 by G Laporte in 1987
Most penalties by a player	2 by G Laporte in 1987

Fiji Cap Match Records

Highest score	16 in 1987
Biggest winning margin	No win
Most tries	2 in 1987
Most points by a player	8 by S Koroduadua in 1987
Most tries by a player	1 by S Daunilatu in 1964
	1 by M Qoro in 1987
	1 by J Damu in 1987
Most conversions by a player	1 by S Koroduadua in 1987
Most penalties by a player	2 by S Koroduadua in 1987

Memorabilia

☐ Michel Crauste (1964) and Daniel Dubroca (1987) led France; Suliasi Cavu (1964) and Koli Rakoroi (1987) captained Fiji.

☐ The matches were controlled by Wales's most distinguished referees: Gwynne Walters (1964) and Clive Norling, who took charge of the 1987 game which was a World Cup quarter final.

☐ Guy Laporte dropped the only goal in the series during the 1987 match.

☐ There has been one other representative match between the countries:

1979   France XV   13–4   Fiji   (Suva)

☐ France, who were returning home from a tour of New Zealand, did not award caps for this match.

☐ Jean-Pierre Rives captained the French side, Costes scored a try and Aguirre (two) and Caussade kicked penalties. Serge Blanco who was then uncapped was an early replacement on the wing for Bustaffa. Prop Peceli Kina scored Fiji's try.

☐ Alan Taylor, a noted New Zealand referee, controlled the match.

☐ Fiji made a tour of France in 1989, winning two and drawing one of their four matches. They defeated the French Barbarians 32–16 but did not play a representative match with a French XV.

CANADA v ROMANIA
Group Four Match   9 October at Toulouse   Kick Off 2000

Major Cap Match Records

NONE

Memorabilia

☐ There has been no previous meeting of the teams at representative level

FRANCE v CANADA
Group Four Match   13 October at Agen   Kick Off 2000

Major Cap Match Records

NONE

Memorabilia

☐ There have been two representative matches but France did not award caps for their previous games with Canada:

1978   France XV   24–9   Canada   (Calgary)
1979   France A   34–15   Canada   (Paris)

☐ The Canadians gave caps for both matches.

☐ The 1978 match took place during a French tour of the Far East and North America. Jean-Pierre Bastiat was the French captain; Bilbao, Bélascain, Novès and Rives scored tries, and Aguirre kicked two penalties and one conversion for France. For Canada prop-forward K J Peace scored a try and scrum-half Wiley converted and kicked a penalty.

☐ Wiley's half-back partner in the 1978 match was John Billingsley, current secretary of the Canadian Rugby Union.

☐ Mike Luke, Canada's hooker and captain in 1978, led his country on a tour of Europe the following season. His side defeated France B (14–4) but were beaten by a strong France A side in Paris.

☐ Alain Caussade kicked 18 points for France A and Serge Blanco was one of the four French try-scorers. For Canada full-back Taylor kicked 8 points, right wing Greig scored a try and Andrew Bibby (who later won an Oxford Blue) dropped a goal.

FIJI v ROMANIA

Group Four Match   12 October at Brive   Kick Off 1900

Major Cap Match Records

NONE

Memorabilia

☐ There has been no previous meeting of the senior teams at representative level

Two Fijian defenders cannot stop John Gallagher, of New Zealand, sprinting away for a try in the 1987 World Cup finals.

THE FIRST WORLD CUP
May/June 1987

by
Stephen Jones

It was a warm autumn in Sydney but there was a sudden icy chill in the air one day in mid-May, 1987. The preparations for the World Cup were complete but in moments of contemplation we all felt anxious. For a start, many diehards – and in rugby, diehards always do die hard – felt that the advent of a World Cup would spell the end of rugby as we know it. Never mind that almost every innovation the game has ever introduced was seen as The End as well and that the whole thing always chugs along onwards and upwards. People were worried.

Never mind the problems of ethos, the perceived dangers. Would the whole thing actually be any good? Would it excite, would there be brilliant rugby, heart-rending moments, big crowds? We felt like the pilot on the Concorde prototype's first venture down the runway – a lot of money and effort had gone into the damn thing but you never really knew if it would lift-off, or whether it would bang its big nose on the ground.

The case was unproven after the first match, in which New Zealand thrashed Italy by 70–6 on a Friday afternoon in Auckland. It was fast-moving stuff and there was a striking long distance try from John Kirwan, the All Blacks' strapping right wing.

But the tournament would hardly be any fun if every little team was pasted

Scrum-half Graeme Bachop gets the New Zealand back line away against Wales.
(from the left) Richard Loe, Gary Whetton, Murray Pierce and Buck Shelford keep a
close eye on proceedings and shield Bachop.

and three-quarters of the games were processional. Then, a glorious two days of rugby, forty-eight hours which changed the game irrevocably – probably the most glorious two days in the sport's history. They banished every single doubt and the events are well worth recounting before even beginning with the discussion and the plaudits for the latter stages and for the eventual victory of the mighty All Black machine.

Back to the opening days. Suddenly, we knew that everything was going to be all right. In one afternoon, the World Cup grew up from tentative, dodgy childhood into manhood and established itself on a four-year cycle for the foreseeable future. It was going to be all right.

I remember vividly sitting in the media centre of the Concord Oval, then the Sydney home of Australian rugby, and watching New Zealand TV's coverage of Romania playing Zimbabwe from Auckland and then France playing Scotland from Christchurch; and then, with the attention switching to our side of the Tasman, I took my seat in the stand to watch Australia play England.

The day left a burning glow. Each of the three games had its own brilliance. The Zimbabweans, practically unknown and infants on the World stage, led Romania by two clear scores inside the final quarter. Their brilliant centre, Richard Tsimba, scored two smashing tries. There was a dramatic end when Romania came back and won by a point, with Zimbabwe hampered by the fact that Tsimba had injured himself in a joyful, exuberant dive for one of his tries and disastrously ruled himself out of the rest of the tournament. The heart ached for the Zimbabweans.

Yet it was all too fast for tears – France and Scotland came out and once again, emotions gushed. Scotland began brilliantly; France, clear favourites and the reigning European champions, came storming back to win. There was controversial refereeing and, eventually, a 20–20 draw. Scotland tried to come to terms with their feelings. It was a magnificent result but tragically, they lost John Rutherford, one of the best Scottish backs ever to lace a boot, with injury. At intervals in play, the camera picked up Rutherford hunched in misery on the bench. He knew, already, that his World Cup was over. Then, large as life, Australia and England came out on to Concord Oval and played a passionate, skilful and deeply controversial match. Australia won by 19–6 but they were never that much better and they knew as well as anyone that the

Serge Blanco uses his left arm to keep Sean Lineen, the Scotland centre, away from the ball. Lhermet (right) adds his support to the French captain's attempt to win possession.

The Scotland front row of Burnell, Milne and Sole are ready to lock horns with the French while Henri Sanz, the scrum-half, is ready to feed the ball for France.

match was decided when Keith Lawrence, New Zealand's referee, awarded a try to David Campese when the brilliant Australian clearly dropped the ball and threw it forward at least two feet off the ground.

The first day had everything. It was a wringer for the emotions but it was to prove only a taster. The very next day, with attention switching to New Zealand, there were three memorable back-to-back matches which a world-wide audience on TV was able to lap up either in highlights or live. First, we saw a striking performance from Napier as Canada, disposing of Tonga with élan and power and by 37–4; when the whistle blew, they could not contain a sense of delirious excitement.

Then the first real shock and, again, a match flooded with emotion. Shortly before the tournament began the coup in Fiji removed the Prime Minister elect and installed Colonel Rabuka, a Fijian international player himself. When the Fijian anthem was played before their match with Argentina in Hamilton and they performed their Ciba, the traditional call to battle, it was obvious that the Fijians, with passion for their homeland at a new fever pitch, had come to play. In a blur of movement and sleight of hand, with four gorgeous tries by Gale, Rokoroi, Nalaga and Savai, they reduced Argentina to a wreck of a side, found a place in the very heart of the tournament and went on to run France close in the rarefied atmosphere of the quarter-finals.

And finally, back in Australia in the colourful Ballymore stadium, Japan and the United States fought a marvellous gripping, waxing-and-waning battle in which the United States got home with a late score. So, after just three days of competition we knew that the World Cup, the meteor, was with us for all time.

There were drawbacks in that marvellous month of rugby. For a start, the fact that the Australian and New Zealand Unions had made all the running in the organisation and, in fact, had kicked out the long-term opposition of the Four Home Unions of the United Kingdom to the whole concept, meant that they simply had to be given joint-host status. This caused logistical problems and in Australia it caused the event to be somewhat lost. Only one of the groups was held in Australia together with two quarter-finals and the two semi-finals. If all the tournament had been held in Australia, or if New Zealand had staged the whole thing, then the focus and the attention would have been greater.

There was also criticism of the commercial operations, the fairly low income from sponsorship and merchandising and from the sale of TV rights. Yet the tournament was arranged at speed, and the arrangers were fumbling in the dark or at best in the unknown. The organisers at least gave the players the chance to establish the tournament and the players, as they tend to do in these matters in any sport, took up the challenge marvellously. Granted, there was no financial windfall handed down and that meant the qualifying events for the 1991 tournament were grossly underfunded, a situation which must never be allowed to happen again. After all, the top IRB inner-sanctum can always stage some money-spinning occasion when they want a few fast bucks. Granted, too, there was no infra-structure handed on for future tournaments. Even the recommendations from the first event were ignored when, improbably, the 1991 tournament was awarded to five countries even though the recommended number was *one*. But what was handed down was credibility; galloping, raging, 24-carat credibility.

It was no fault of the Australians but the heart and the soul of the World Cup resided in New Zealand. This was graphically illustrated on the first Saturday night of the tournament. Some of us left Australia behind rather bemoaning the fact that the man in the street was showing only passing interest, that there were other major sports in Sydney and Brisbane. That changed almost as soon as the trans-Tasman flight touched down at Christchurch, that gleaming, splendid New Zealand city, at midnight on a cold Kiwi night. Suddenly, despite the hour, the World Cup became overwhelming. The customs officers wanted to talk about it; the lady in the money-change desk, the taxi drivers, the hotel receptionist, every city Kiwi and every redneck country Kiwi bumpkin. And being New Zealand, they were a stage beyond merely asking you how the games would go. They wanted to talk about Grant Fox's tactical appreciation and John Kirwan's lines of running.

What really made the tournament for me was the reaction to it from the large crowds at places like Palmerston North, Invercargill and Hamilton. Even for the apparently meaningless third place match in the week before the final, there was a massive, thunderously noisy gathering in Rotorua to see Wales and Australia do battle in a match decided by a brilliant late Welsh try and a stupendous conversion from the touch-line by Paul Thorburn. The crowd, uproarious Welshmen for a day, made enough noise for an international gathering.

The home countries never really left their stamp on the competition. The lack of glorious moments and brilliant players in the matches involving them was unacceptable and, above anything, provided the spur to knock the preparations into better shape for the 1991 event. Admittedly, England looked large, fit and promising before the tournament as they worked up; trying to ignore the barrage of publicity for the other seeded team in their group, the Australians. The host side and especially their coach, the ferociously-vociferous Alan Jones, lost no time at all in scoring propaganda points and emphasising that the other teams in the tournament were turning up to make up the numbers. It was an attitude which was to hurt the Aussie team later because they found that the whole of the rest of the tournament ganged up on them.

Jersey pulling Welsh style. The Western Samoan lock (No 5) attempts to help keep his team mate's jersey on his back in Cardiff.

However, the Australians came through the group, defeating England with infinitely less ease than the 19–6 scoreline suggested. England safely coasted through their other qualifying games, crushing Japan by 60–7 and the USA by 34–6. There seemed to be a hard core to the pack with Wade Dooley and Dean Richards at the front, the talented Peter Williams at fly-half seemed to be growing into his role and all Australia saw red for danger whenever Rory Underwood was in possession.

Over in New Zealand, Wales were advancing steadily on a quarter-final meeting with England, something which both sides desperately tried not to make an obsession – and failed. Wales comfortably disposed of a desperately disappointing Ireland in a match ruined by the strong wind at Athletic Park, Wellington, the town of the perma-hurricane. Ireland hit the ground shambling, losing 13–6 against a splendid display of tactical kicking by Jonathan Davies and there were signs that the likes of John Devereux in the centre, Stuart Evans and Bob Norster in the pack, could weld the team into something outstanding. It turned out that the team was to be hit savagely hard

John Devereux, another Welsh player who has turned to rugby league since the 1987 tournament. Here he gets the ball away with England's Gary Rees and Brian Moore (headband) showing their total commitment to the tackle.

by injury and by the end over half of their opening top side were unavailable. It made a mockery of early promise even though Wales were to finish in third place in the tournament.

Wales and Ireland still reached the quarter-finals. Wales had stiff resistance to overcome, gaining victories over Tonga and Canada. The first of these matches saw the giant Stuart Evans out of the tournament and the second saw some superlative running from Jonathan Davies, a treasure of the tournament even though the opposition was not from the top drawer. Ireland beat Canada 46–19; but the final score gives no indication that until a clinical late Irish surge the result was in the balance. They went on to see off the Tongans and set off for Australia and a quarter-final against the awesome Australians.

Neither Scotland nor France had problems in clearing up the rest of the group with victories over Zimbabwe and Romania, the latter a team which had fallen rapidly from its position of eminence in the early-1980s and which was to fall even further in matches after the tournament. The New Zealanders stormed through their group, probably the easiest due to the collapse of Argentina and the fact that when the All Blacks met Fiji, the Fijians were thinking about the latter stages and fielded only a weakened, token side. The quarter-finals, therefore, panned out roughly as predicted, with Australia v Ireland, France v Fiji, Wales v England and New Zealand v Scotland.

The fight for the semi-finals was thunderous, and also flawed. Australia shook Ireland to the bottom of their studs with a powerful opening passage in which they threatened to score 60 points but tailed off to win 33–15, with brilliant play from Brett Papworth in the centre and conspicuous resistance from Neil Francis and Phil Matthews. Ireland departed without ever doing themselves justice and apparently falling between at least three tactical stools.

The France-Fiji match went to France 31–16 but there were times when the brilliant Fijians threatened to cause the greatest upset of all in world rugby history. Forwards like Rakai and Savai showed hard-running, deft Fijian rugby in all its glory and Fiji threatened to draw level late in the game when another spectacular Fijian burst left Koroduadua free with the line approaching. However, to the horror of every non-Frenchman watching from any vantage point throughout the world, he held the ball in one extended fist and it simply popped out and away as he chose his spot for the touchdown. It was a stupendously gauche error, one which would have earned an All Black a dressing down followed by a firing squad. France, drawing on the power of Sella and Mesnel in the centre and with the forbidding Garuet anchoring the scrum, gathered themselves and took the semi-final place they clearly deserved.

Wales' victory over England, after a match of desperate tension and halting rugby in Brisbane, once again exposed cruelly the inner turmoil in which England find themselves when they meet their bitterest enemy. England were outwardly composed as they prepared and in many respects Wales were a shambles. Norster, their line-out hero, was roughly half-fit and such were the injury problems up front that Wales even had to draft in David Young, a 19-year-old prop just old enough to qualify as an infant on the international stage. Young had been holidaying in Canberra, playing a little local rugby. Now he was pitched into the furnace heat of the World Cup's latter stages. It should have been no contest. Yet in the first scrum, incredibly, Wales drove forward a yard, a massive boost to morale. England never recovered. The only source of possession was a stream of penalties awarded in their favour and three Welsh tries, from Roberts, Devereux and Robert Jones, saw Wales through.

It was a watershed for both teams. Wales staggered on even more beleaguered by injury to a semi-final thrashing at the hands of New Zealand, a day of pain during which Huw Richards was sent off, with Wayne Shelford of New Zealand desperately lucky not to join him. The result affected Welsh rugby, mentally and otherwise, so badly that they have not fully recovered even four years later. England reacted to the defeat by sacking their coaches, by instituting a more professional approach and by working hard on mental preparation. It was no use building a talented team if it became mush inside simply because of one scrum.

Scotland at least offered stern resistance in their quarter-final with New Zealand and the Scots were also hit by injuries. Yet there was never a time when Scotland were going to win or even run the home team close and a 30–3 scoreline did not really do the All Blacks justice. There was play of real power from the likes of McDowell and Fitzpatrick in the front row and from the Whettons, Alan and Gary, further back. Colin Deans, a marvellously inspirational Scottish captain, declared that the New Zealand pack was the most powerful he had ever played against.

If the New Zealand-Wales semi-final was remarkable only for the size of the thrashing and for the evidence that a wonderful sporting rivalry was now devalued because it was no contest, then the other was something else altogether. The Australia-France match went down (in the immediate aftermath and also after more sober reflection) as the greatest match ever played. The memories are indelible: of the surging nature of the contest, with brilliant tries and harshness in the play; of the Australian crowd at the suburban Concord Oval ground fiercely supporting their men; and of all other nationalities ganging noisily up on the home team.

There was a graphic try from Lorieux, the French lock. Just as the home fans were acclaiming a clean line-out catch from Coker, Lorieux had torn the ball from him, gone surging round the front of the line-out and hurled himself over. Then, the final glorious rush. Franch stormed upfield after a fly-hacked ball, moved it left, switched the ball back to the right and suddenly, the panther Blanco was away down the left wing. He hurled himself at the corner flag in the tackle of Lawton, the Australian hooker. He scored, and by the time

Henri Sanz, the French scrum-half, releases Didier Camberabero in the 1990 meeting with Scotland.

he picked himself up the French team were already in tears of incredulity and joy. It ended at 30–24 and, far more than the final, it was the keynote match of the World Cup itself.

France left much of their game in Sydney. In the final, which New Zealand won 29–9 and deserved every point, they were flat and uninspired and for everyone bar the delirious country of New Zealand it was similarly downbeat. There was a wonderful sense of occasion about Eden Park, Auckland but the All Blacks were too good, too committed. Their captain, David Kirk, appropriately scored one of the tries and the others came from key men too – Michael Jones, the flanker and John Kirwan, the unstoppable. It was also appropriate that the country which had fought for the tournament, which had sweated blood in preparing for it, should win it.

And that was that – apart, that is, from acclaiming a dramatic, thrilling, overwhelming and unforgettable victory for the sport itself.

Stephen Jones is rugby correspondent for the *Sunday Times*

THE 1991 WORLD CUP QUALIFYING TOURAMENT RESULTS

The face of a world-class wing in full flight as Rory Underwood, England's try scorer, attacks for the Lions in Australia in 1989. Underwood is now recognised as one of rugby's great finishers and his ability to break through the toughest defences was vitally important to England's 1991 Grand Slam campaign.

AFRICAN ZONE QUALIFYING TOURNAMENT

5 May 1990	Morocco	12–16	Tunisia
5 May 1990	Zimbabwe	22–9	Ivory Coast
8 May 1990	Tunisia	12–7	Ivory Coast
8 May 1990	Zimbabwe	16–0	Morocco
12 May 1990	Tunisia	13–24	Zimbabwe
12 May 1990	Morocco	11–4	Ivory Coast

	P	W	D	L	For	Against	Pts
Zimbabwe	3	3	0	0	62	22	6
Tunisia	3	2	0	1	41	43	4
Morocco	3	1	0	2	23	36	2
Ivory Coast	3	0	0	3	20	45	0

(One Qualifier)

ZIMBABWE

v. IVORY COAST

M. Cremer

Z. Dzinomurumbi
M. Letcher
D. Walters
E. Chimbima

R. Kuhn
* A. Ferreira

R. Moore
P. Albasini
A. Garvey
B. Matthewman
A. Horton
N. Bushell
H. Nguruve
B. Dawson

Harare
WON 22–9

Scorers
D. Walters 1T
E. Chimbima 1T
R. Kuhn 1DG
A. Ferreira 3PG, 1C

5 May 1990

v. MOROCCO

A. Rex

Z. Dzinomurumbi
M. Letcher
M. Cremer
E. Chimbima

D. Walters
* A. Ferreira

R. Moore
P. Albasini
A. Garvey[1]
B. Matthewman
A. Horton
N. Bushell
H. Nguruve
B. Dawson

Harare
WON 16–0

Scorers
Z. Dzinomurumbi 1T
A. Ferreira 1T, 2PG, 1C

9 May 1990

v. TUNISIA

A. Rex

Z. Dzinomurumbi
M. Letcher
M. Cremer
E. Chimbima

D. Walters
* A. Ferreira

R. Moore
P. Albasini
W. Cornish
B. Matthewman
A. Horton
N. Bushell
H. Nguruve
B. Dawson

Harare
WON 24–13

Scorers
Z. Dzinomurumbi 1T
A. Ferreira 1T, 4PG, 2C

12 May 1990

[1] Rep by G. Davidson

Key
* captain

223

AMERICAS ZONE QUALIFYING TOURNAMENT

23 Sep 1989	Canada	21–3	United States
8 Nov 1989	Argentina	23–6	United States
30 Mar 1990	Canada	15–6	Argentina
7 Apr 1990	United States	6–13	Argentina
9 Jun 1990	United States	14–12	Canada
16 Jun 1990	Argentina	15–19	Canada

	P	W	D	L	For	Against	Pts
Canada	4	3	0	1	67	38	6
Argentina	4	2	0	2	57	46	4
United States	4	1	0	3	29	69	2

(All Qualify)

ARGENTINA

v. UNITED STATES	v. CANADA	v. UNITED STATES	v. CANADA
A.A. Scolni	A.A. Scolni	A.A. Scolni	P. Garzon
F. Schacht	F. Schacht	D. Halle	D. Cuesta Silva
M.H. Loffreda	* M.H. Loffreda	* M.H. Loffreda	S. Salvat
S. Meson	S. Salvat	S. Meson	M. Allen
C.I. Mendy	R. Zanero	S. Salvat	C.I. Mendy
D. Halle	H. Vidou	H. Vidou	S. Meson
F. Silvestre	F. Silvestre	F. Silvestre	E.F. Gomez
D.M. Cash	D.M. Cash	D.M. Cash	A.S. Rocca
J.J. Angelillo	J.J. Angelillo	J.J. Angelillo	D.M. Cash
A.S. Rocca	A.S. Rocca	A.S. Rocca	L.E. Molina
M. Valesani	M. Valesani	M. Valesani	M. Valesani
P. Buabse	J. Grondona[1]	J. Simes[1]	* A. Iachetti
P.A. Garreton	P. di Nisio	P. di Nisio	P.A. Garreton
S. Bunader	P. Camerlinckx	M. Baeck	S. Bunader
* J.G. Allen	M.J.S. Bertranou	M.J.S. Bertranou	M.J.S. Bertranou
Velez Sarsfield, B.A.	Burnaby, Vancouver	Santa Barbara	Velez Sarsfield, B.A.
WON 23–6	LOST 6–15	WON 13–6	LOST 15–19

Scorers	*Scorer*	*Scorers*	*Scorers*
M.H. Loffreda 1T	H. Vidou 2PG	M.H. Loffreda 1T	P. Garzon 1T
S. Meson 3PG,		H. Vidou 1PG, 1C	S. Meson 1PG
1T, 1C			S. Bunader 2T
S. Bunader 1T			

8 Nov 1989	30 Mar 1990	7 Apr 1990	16 Jun 1990
	[1] Rep by J. Simes	[1] Rep by P. Camerlinckx 1T	

225

CANADA

v. UNITED STATES

D.S. Stewart

M.A. Wyatt
I.C. Stuart
S.T.T. Brown
T.A. Woods

G.L. Rees[1]
J.D. Graf

E.A. Evans
D.A. Speirs
P. Szabo
J.R. Robertsen
N. Hadley
R.E. Radu
* G.D. Ennis
G.I. MacKinnon

Toronto
WON 21–3

Scorers
M.A. Wyatt 1C, 5PG
S.T.T. Brown 1T

23 Sep 1989

[1] Rep by R.P. Ross

v. ARGENTINA

* M.A. Wyatt

P. Palmer
I.C. Stuart
T.A. Woods
S.D. Gray

G.L. Rees
C.J. Tynan

E.A. Evans
K.F. Svoboda
P. Szabo
R.E. Hindson
J.R. Robertsen
A.J. Charron[1]
G.D. Ennis
G.I. MacKinnon

Burnaby
WON 15–6

Scorers
M.A. Wyatt 3PG, 1C
P. Palmer 1T

30 Mar 1990

[1] Rep by R.E. Radu

v. UNITED STATES

* M.A. Wyatt

P. Palmer
T.A. Woods
I.C. Stuart
S.D. Gray

R.P. Ross
C.J. Tynan

G.A. Dukelow
K.F. Svoboda
P. Szabo
J.R. Robertsen
C. Fowler
A.J. Charron
G.D. Ennis
B. Breen

Seattle
LOST 12–14

Scorers
M.A. Wyatt 1PG, 1C
R.P. Ross 1DG
G.D. Ennis 1T

9 Jun 1990

v. ARGENTINA

* M.A. Wyatt[1]

S.D. Gray
D.C. Lougheed
I.C. Stuart
J.D. Graf

G.L. Rees
C.J. Tynan

E.A. Evans
K.F. Svoboda
P. Szabo
A.J. Charron
N. Hadley
G.I. MacKinnon
J.R. Robertsen[2]
R.E. Radu

Buenos Aires
WON 19–15

Scorers
I.C. Stuart 1T
G.L. Rees 4PG, 1DG

16 Jun 1990

[1] Rep by D.S. Stewart
[2] Rep by G.D. Ennis

226

UNITED STATES

v. CANADA   v. ARGENTINA   v. ARGENTINA   v. CANADA

v. CANADA	v. ARGENTINA	v. ARGENTINA	v. CANADA
A. Montgomery	R. Nelson	R. Nelson	R. Nelson
B. Williams	G. Hein	G. Hein	C. Lewis
K. Higgins	M. Williams[3]	M. Williams	M. Williams
C. O'Brien	* K. Higgins	* K. Higgins	J. Burke
G. Hein	B. Corcoran	B. Corcoran	C. Williams
M. Caulder	C. O'Brien	C. O'Brien	M. DeJong
* M. Saunders	B. Daily	B. Daily	B. Daily
C. Lippert	C. Lippert[2]	C. Lippert	C. Lippert
P. Johnson	T. McCormack[1]	T. McCormack	T. McCormack
F. Paoli	F. Paoli	N. Mottram	D. James
R. Issac	R. Issac	K. Swords	K. Swords
K. Swords	K. Swords	W. Leversee	W. Leversee
M. Siano	M. Siano	M. Sawicki	S. Lipman
G. Lambert	G. Lambert	G. Lambert	* B. Vizard
B. Vizard	R. Farley	R. Farley	R. Farley
Varsity Stadium, Toronto	Velez Sarsfield, B.A.	Santa Barbara, Calif.	Seattle
LOST 3–21	LOST 6–23	LOST 6–13	WON 14–12

Scorer	*Scorer*	*Scorers*	*Scorers*
C. O'Brien 1PG	C. O'Brien 2PG	C. O'Brien 1C	C. Lewis 1T
		W. Leversee 1T	M. Williams 1PG
			M. DeJong 1PG
			B. Daily 1T
23 Sep 1989	8 Nov 1989	7 Apr 1990	9 Jun 1990

[1] Rep by P. Johnson
[2] Rep by A. Manga
[3] Rep by S. LaPorta

227

EUROPEAN ZONE QUALIFYING TOURNAMENT

30 Sep 1990	Italy	30–6	Spain
30 Sep 1990	Romania	45–7	Holland
3 Oct 1990	Italy	24–11	Holland
3 Oct 1990	Romania	19–6	Spain
7 Oct 1990	Italy	29–21	Romania
7 Oct 1990	Spain	22–12	Holland

	P	W	D	L	For	Against	Pts
Italy	3	3	0	0	83	38	6
Romania	3	2	0	1	85	42	4
Spain	3	1	0	2	34	61	2
Holland	3	0	0	3	30	91	0

(Two Qualifiers)

ITALY

v. SPAIN

L. Troiani

E. Venturi
S. Barba
Fabio Gaetaniello
M. Brunello

M. Bonomi
U. Casellato

Massimo Cuttitta
G. Pivetta
F. Properzi-Curti
G. Croci
C. Checchinato
R. Saetti
* G. Zanon
M. Giovanelli

Rovigo
WON 30–6

Scorers
L. Troiani 2C, 5PG
E. Venturi 1T
M. Bonomi 1DG
M. Giovanelli 1T

30 Sep 1990

v. HOLLAND

L. Troiani

E. Venturi
S. Barba
Fabio Gaetaniello
M. Brunello

M. Bonomi
F. Pietrosanti

Massimo Cuttitta
M. Goti
F. Properzi-Curti
R. Favaro
G. Croci
R. Saetti
* G. Zanon
M. Giovanelli

Treviso
WON 24–11

Scorers
L. Troiani 5PG, 1C
S. Barba 1T
M. Bonomi 1DG

3 Oct 1990

v. ROMANIA

L. Troiani

E. Venturi
S. Bordon
S. Barba
M. Brunello

M. Bonomi
I. Francescato

Massimo Cuttitta
G. Pivetta
F. Properzi-Curti[1]
R. Favaro
G. Croci
R. Saetti
* G. Zanon
M. Giovanelli

Padua
WON 29–21

Scorers
L. Troiani 2PG, 1C
M. Brunello 1DG, 1T
M. Bonomi 2DG
I. Francescato 1T
R. Saetti 1T

7 Oct 1990

[1] Rep by G. Grespan

229

ROMANIA

v. HOLLAND	v. SPAIN	v. ITALY
M. Dumitru	M. Dumitru	M. Dumitru
S. Chirila	S. Chirila	S. Chirila[2]
N. Fulina	N. Fulina	G. Sava
G. Sava	G. Sava	A. Lungu
N. Racean	N. Racean	N. Racean
G. Ignat	G. Ignat[1]	N. Nichitean
D. Neaga	D. Neaga	S. Seceleanu
G. Dumitrescu	G. Dumitrescu	G. Dumitrescu
G. Ion	G. Ion	* G. Ion[3]
G. Leonte	G. Leonte	G. Leonte
C. Cojocariu	C. Cojocariu	C. Cojocariu
S. Ciorascu	S. Ciorascu	T. Oroian[1]
G. Dinu	G. Dinu	G. Dinu
* H. Dumitras[1]	* H. Dumitras	T. Brinza
A. Radulescu	A. Radulescu	I. Doja
Treviso	Padua	Padua
WON 45–7	WON 19–6	LOST 21–29

Scorers	Scorers	Scorers
M. Dumitru 1DG	N. Racean 1T	N. Nichitean 1DG, 4PG, 1C
S. Chirila 1T	G. Ignat 1DG	A. Radulescu 1T
N. Racean 2T	H. Dumitras 1T	
G. Ignat 5C, 4PG	N. Nichitean 2PG, 1C	
C. Cojocariu 1T		
H. Dumitras 1T		

30 Sep 1990	3 Oct 1990	7 Oct 1990

[1] Rep by C. Stan	[1] Rep by N. Nichitean	[1] Rep by A. Radulescu
		[2] Rep by M. Toader
		[3] Rep by V. Tufa

SOUTH PACIFIC ZONE QUALIFYING TOURNAMENT

8 Apr 1990	Korea	7–74	Western Samoa
8 Apr 1990	Japan	28–16	Tonga
11 Apr 1990	Tonga	3–12	Western Samoa
11 Apr 1990	Japan	26–10	Korea
15 Apr 1990	Tonga	45–22	Korea
15 Apr 1990	Japan	11–37	Western Samoa

	P	W	D	L	For	Against	Pts
Western Samoa	3	3	0	0	123	21	6
Japan	3	2	0	1	65	63	4
Tonga	3	1	0	2	64	62	2
Korea	3	0	0	3	39	145	0

(Two Qualify)

JAPAN

v. TONGA

T. Hosokawa

T. Goda
E. Kutsuki
* S. Hirao
Y. Yoshida

K. Matsuo
M. Horikoshi

O. Ota
T. Fujita
M. Takura
T. Hayashi
A. Oyagi
H. Kajihara
S. T. Latu
S. Nakashima

Tokyo
WON 28–16[††]

Scorers
T. Hosokawa 1C, 6PG
Y. Yoshida 1T

8 Apr 1990

[††] Japan scored a penalty try

v. KOREA

T. Hosokawa

T. Goda
E. Kutsuki
* S. Hirao
Y. Yoshida

K. Matsuo
M. Horikoshi

O. Ota
T. Fujita
M. Takura
A. Oyagi
E. Luaiufi
H. Kajihara
S. T. Latu
S. Nakashima

Tokyo
WON 26–10

Scorers
T. Hosokawa 2C, 2PG, 2T
Y. Yoshida 1T
S.T. Latu 1T

11 Apr 1990

v. WESTERN SAMOA

T. Hosokawa

T. Goda
K. Yoshinaga
E. Kutsuki
Y. Yoshida

K. Matsuo
H. Watanabe

O. Ota[1]
* T. Fujita[2]
M. Takura
T. Hayashi
A. Oyagi
H. Kajihara
S. T. Latu
S. Nakashima

Tokyo
LOST 11–37

Scorers
T. Hosokawa 1PG
Y. Yoshida 1T
T. Fujita 1T

15 Apr 1990

[1] Rep by K. Takahashi
[2] Rep by M. Kunda

WESTERN SAMOA

v. KOREA

A. Aiolupo

T. Tagaloa
T. Manoo
J. Ah Kuoi
T. Faamasino

P.D. Saena
M. Moke

* P. Fatialofa
S. Toomalati
A. Leuu
P. Fuatai
S.P. Ching
S. Vaifale
H. Schuster
D. Kaleope

Tokyo
WON 74–7

Scorers
A. Aiolupo 1T, 8C, 1PG
T. Tagaloa 2T
T. Manoo 1T
J. Ah Kuoi 1DG
T. Faamasino 3T
P.D. Saena 1T
S. Toomalati 1T
S. Vaifale 2T
H. Schuster 1T
D. Kaleope 1T

8 Apr 1990

v. TONGA

A. Aiolupo

T. Tagaloa
T. Manoo
J. Ah Kuoi
T. Faamasino

P.D. Saena
M. Moke

* P. Fatialofa
S. Toomalati
T. Sio
S.P. Ching
P. Fuatai
S. Vaifale
H. Schuster
D. Kaleope

Tokyo
WON 12–3

Scorers
A. Aiolupo 1C, 2PG
P. Fatialofa 1T

11 Apr 1990

v. JAPAN

A. Aiolupo

T. Tagaloa
T. Manoo
K. Sio
T. Faamasino

P.D. Saena
M. Moke

* P. Fatialofa
S. Toomalati
A. Leuu
P. Leavai
P. Fuatai[1]
S. Vaifale
H. Schuster
D. Kaleope

Tokyo
WON 37–11

Scorers
A. Aiolupo 5C, 1PG
T. Tagaloa 1T
T. Manoo 1T
S. Toomalati 1T
A. Leuu 1T
S. Vaifale 1T
D. Kaleope 1T

15 Apr 1990

1987 WORLD CUP RECORDS

LEADING SCORERS

Most Points in the Competition

126	G.J.Fox	New Zealand
82	M.P. Lynagh	Australia
62	A.G. Hastings	Scotland

Most Conversions in the Competition

30	G.J. Fox	New Zealand
20	M.P. Lynagh	Australia
16	A.G. Hastings	Scotland

Most Tries in the Competition

6	C.I. Green	New Zealand
6	J.J. Kirwan	New Zealand
5	M.E. Harrison	England
5	D.E. Kirk	New Zealand
5	A.J. Whetton	New Zealand
5	J.A. Gallagher	New Zealand
5	M.P. Burke	Australia

Most Penalty Goals in the Competition

21	G.J. Fox	New Zealand
12	M.P. Lynagh	Australia

Most Dropped Goals in the Competition

3	J. Davies	Wales
2	O. Collodo	Italy
2	M.P. Lynagh	Australia

Most Points in a Match

By a team

74	New Zealand v Fiji	Christchurch
70	New Zealand v Italy	Auckland
70	France v Zimbabwe	Auckland
60	England v Japan	Sydney
60	Scotland v Zimbabwe	Wellington

By a Player

30	D. Camberabero	France v Zimbabwe	Auckland
27	A.G. Hastings	Scotland v Romania	Dunedin
26	G.J. Fox	New Zealand v Fiji	Christchurch
23	G. Laporte	France v Romania	Wellington
22	G.J. Fox	New Zealand v Italy	Auckland
22	G.J. Fox	New Zealand v Argentina	Wellington
22	G.J. Fox	New Zealand v Scotland	Christchurch

Most Tries in a Match

By a team

13	France v Zimbabwe	Auckland
12	New Zealand v Italy	Auckland
12	New Zealand v Fiji	Christchurch
11	Scotland v Zimbabwe	Wellington

By a player

4	I.C. Evans	Wales v Canada	Invercargill
4	C.I. Green	New Zealand v Fiji	Christchurch
4	J.A. Gallagher	New Zealand v Fiji	Christchurch

Most Conversions in a Match

By a team

10	New Zealand v Fiji	Christchurch
9	France v Zimbabwe	Auckland
8	New Zealand v Italy	Auckland
8	France v Romania	Wellington
8	Scotland v Zimbabwe	Wellington
8	Scotland v Romania	Dunedin

By a player

10	G.J. Fox	New Zealand v Fiji	Christchurch
9	D. Camberabero	France v Zimbabwe	Auckland
8	G.J. Fox	New Zealand v Italy	Auckland
8	G. Laporte	France v Romania	Wellington
8	A.G. Hastings	Scotland v Zimbabwe	Wellington
8	A.G. Hastings	Scotland v Romania	Dunedin

Most Penalty Goals in a Match

By a team

6	New Zealand v Scotland	Christchurch
6	New Zealand v Argentina	Wellington
5	Argentina v Italy	Christchurch
5	Zimbabwe v Scotland	Wellington

By a player

6	G.J. Fox	New Zealand v Scotland	Christchurch
6	G.J. Fox	New Zealand v Argentina	Wellington
5	H. Porta	Argentina v Italy	Christchurch
5	M. Grobler	Zimbabwe v Scotland	Wellington

Most Dropped Goals in a Match

By a team

2	Wales v Ireland	Wellington
2	Ireland v Canada	Dunedin

By a player

2	J. Davies	Wales v Ireland	Wellington

ABOVE: *Scotland's Gavin Hastings kicked eight conversions in two matches during the 1987 World Cup finals.*

PREVIOUS PAGE: *Simon Hodgkinson, the England full-back, who kicked a world record seven penalties against Wales this year.*

POOL ONE

	P	W	D	L	For	Against	Pts
Australia	3	3	0	0	108	41	6
England	3	2	0	1	100	32	4
United States	3	1	0	2	39	99	2
Japan	3	0	0	3	48	123	0

AUSTRALIA v. ENGLAND

Date: 23 May 1987   Venue: Concord Oval, Sydney
19–6

AUSTRALIA	ENGLAND
1G, 3PG, 1T	1G

R.G. Gould[1]; P.C. Grigg, *A.G. Slack, B. Papworth, D.I. Campese; M.P. Lynagh, N.C. Farr-Jones; E.E. Rodriguez, T.A. Lawton, A.J. McIntyre, S.A.G. Cutler, W.A. Campbell, S.P. Poidevin, †T. Coker, S.N. Tuynman

[1] Rep by S.L. James

Tries: Campese, Poidevin
Cons: Lynagh
PG: Lynagh (3)
DG: –

W.M.H. Rose[1]; *M.E. Harrison, K.G. Simms, J.L.B. Salmon, R. Underwood; P.N. Williams, R.M. Harding; P.A.G. Rendall, B.C. Moore, G.S. Pearce, W.A. Dooley, N.C. Redman, P.J. Winterbottom, D. Richards, G.W. Rees

[1]Rep by †J. Webb

Tries: Harrison
Cons: Webb
PG: –
DG: –

Referee: K.H. Lawrence (NZ)

Key   † new cap awarded to a player from an international board country

JAPAN v. UNITED STATES

Date: 24 May 1987   Venue: Ballymore, Brisbane
18–21

JAPAN	UNITED STATES
2PG, 3T	3G, 1PG

S. Mukai; N. Taumoefolau, K. Yoshinaga,
E. Kutusuki, S. Onuki; S. Hirao, H. Ikuta;
H. Yasumi, T. Fujita, K. Horaguchi,
*T. Hayashi, A. Oyagi, K. Miyamoto, M. Chida,
S. Latu

R. Nelson; M. Purcell, K. Higgins, R. Helu,
G. Hein; J. Clarkson, M. Saunders; R. Bailey,
J. Everett, F. Paoli, K. Swords,
*E. Burlingham, B. Warhurst, B. Vizard,
G. Lambert

Tries: Taumoefolau (2), Yoshinaga
Cons: –
PG: Yoshinaga, Kutsuki
DG: –

Tries: Nelson, Purcell, Lambert
Cons: Nelson (3)
PG: Nelson
DG: –

Referee: G. Maurette (France)

ENGLAND v. JAPAN

Date: 30 May 1987   Venue: Concord Oval, Sydney
60–7

ENGLAND	JAPAN
7G, 2PG, 3T	1PG, 1T

J. Webb; *M.E. Harrison, K.G. Simms[1],
J.L.B. Salmon, R. Underwood; P.N. Williams[2],
R.M. Harding; P.A.G. Rendall, B.C. Moore,
G.J. Chilcott, N.C. Redman, S.Bainbridge,
P.J. Winterbottom, D. Richards, G.W. Rees

D. Murai; N. Taumoefolau, E. Kutsuki,
K. Matsuo, S. Onuki; S. Hirao, M. Hagimoto;
T. Kimura, T. Fujita, K. Horaguchi,
S. Kurihara, A. Oyagi, K. Miyamoto, M. Chida,
*T. Hayashi

[1]Rep. by F.J. Clough
[2]Rep. by C.R. Andrew

Tries: Underwood (2), Rees, Harrison (3),
  Salmon, Richards, Simms, Redman
Cons: Webb (7)
PG: Webb (2)
DG: –

Tries: Miyamoto
Cons: –
PG: Matsuo
DG: –

Referee: R. Hourquet (France)

AUSTRALIA v. UNITED STATES

Date: 31 May 1987   Venue: Ballymore, Brisbane

47–12

AUSTRALIA	UNITED STATES
6G, 1PG, 2T	1G, 1PG, 1DG

A. Leeds; D.I. Campese, *A.G. Slack,
B. Papworth, M.P. Burke; M.P. Lynagh,
B. Smith; C.A. Lillicrap, T.A. Lawton,
A.J. McIntyre, T. Coker, W.A. Campbell,
D. Codey, S.N. Tuynman, J.S. Miller

Tries: Leeds (2), Slack, Smith, Papworth,
  Codey, Campese, Penalty try
Cons: Lynagh (6)
PG: Lynagh
DG: –

R. Nelson; K. Higgins, R. Helu, T. Vinick,
G. Hein; D. Horton, D. Dickson[1]; F. Horwath,
P. Johnson, *F. Paoli, K. Swords, W. Shiflet[2],
A. Ridnell, B. Vizard, S. Finkel

[1]Rep. by M. Saunders
[2]Rep. by G. Lambert

Tries: Nelson
Cons: Nelson
PG: Nelson
DG: Horton

Referee: J.B. Anderson (Scotland)

ENGLAND v. UNITED STATES

Date: 3 June 1987   Venue: Concord Oval, Sydney

34–6

ENGLAND	UNITED STATES
3G, 4PG, 1T	1G

J. Webb; *M.E. Harrison, F.J. Clough,
J.L.B. Salmon, M.D. Bailey; C.R. Andrew,
R.J. Hill; G.J. Chilcott, R.G.R. Dawe,
G.S. Pearce, W.A. Dooley, S. Bainbridge,
P.J. Winterbottom, D. Richards, G.W. Rees

Tries: Winterbottom (2), Harrison, Dooley
Cons: Webb (3)
PG: Webb (4)
DG: –

R. Nelson; M. Purcell, K. Higgins, T. Vinick,
G. Hein; J. Clarkson, M. Saunders; R. Bailey,
J. Everett, N. Brendel, R. Causey,
*E. Burlingham, G. Lambert, B. Vizard,
S. Finkel

Tries: Purcell
Cons: Nelson
PG: –
DG: –

Referee: K.V.J. Fitzgerald (Australia)

AUSTRALIA v. JAPAN

Date: 3 June 1987   Venue: Concord Oval, Sydney
42–23

AUSTRALIA	JAPAN
5G, 3T	1G, 1DG, 2PG, 2T

D.I. Campese; P.C. Grigg, A.G. Slack, M.T. Cook[1], M.P. Burke; M.P. Lynagh, B. Smith; E.E. Rodriguez, M.I. McBain, M.N. Hartill, S.A.G. Cutler, R.J. Reynolds, *S.P. Poidevin, S.N. Tuynman[2], D. Codey

S. Mukai; N. Taumoefolau, K. Yoshinaga, E. Kutsuki, M. Okidoi; S. Hirao, H. Ikuta; T. Kimura, T. Fujita, M. Aizawa, *T. Hayashi, Y. Sakuraba, K. Miyamoto, S. Latu, Y. Kawase

[1]Rep. by B. Papworth
[2]Rep. by W.A. Campbell

Tries: Slack (2), Burke (2). Grigg, Tuynman, Hartill, Campese
Cons: Lynagh (5)
PG: –
DG: –

Tries: Kutsuki (2), Fujita
Cons: Okidoi
PG: Okidoi (2)
DG: Okidoi

Referee: J.M. Fleming (Scotland)

OVERLEAF: Mike Harrison, who captained England in the 1987 finals, is airborne after a magnificent tackle by Australia's Brett Papworth. The clash between the teams was one of the most exciting matches of the 1987 World Cup, with Harrison scoring England's only try in a 19–6 defeat at Sydney's Concord Oval stadium.

POOL TWO

	P	W	D	L	For	Against	Pts
Wales	3	3	0	0	82	31	6
Ireland	3	2	0	1	84	41	4
Canada	3	1	0	2	65	90	2
Tonga	3	0	0	3	29	98	0

CANADA v. TONGA

Date: 24 May 1987   Venue: McLean Park, Napier
37–4

CANADA	TONGA
3G, 1PG, 4T	1T

M. Wyatt; P. Palmer, P. Vaesen, S. McTavish,
T. Woods; G. Rees, I. Stuart; E. Evans,
M. Cardinal, W. Handson, *H. de Goede,
R. van den Brink, R. Frame, G. Ennis, R. Radu

Tries: Vaesen (2), Palmer (2), Stuart, Frame,
   Penalty try
Cons: Wyatt (2), Rees
PG: Rees
DG: –

T. Ete'aki; S. Asi[1], S. Mohi,
T. Fukakitekei'aho, K. Fielea; A. Liava'a,
T. Fifita; S. Motu'apuaka, A. Afu Fungavaka,
H. Tupou, P. Tui'halamaka[2], K. Fine,
V. Tu'uta Kakato, K. Fotu, *F. Valu

[1]Rep. by L. Vaipulu
[2]Rep. by S. Tahaafe

Tries: Valu
Cons: –
PG: –
DG: –

Referee: C. Norling (Wales)

IRELAND v. WALES

Date: 25 May 1987   Venue: Athletic Park, Wellington
6–13

IRELAND	WALES
2PG	**1PG, 2DG, 1T**

H.P. MacNeill; T.M. Ringland, B.J. Mullin, M.J. Kiernan, K.D. Crossan; P.M. Dean, M.T. Bradley; P.A. Orr, †T. Kingston, D.C. Fitzgerald, *D.G. Lenihan, W.A. Anderson, P.M. Matthews[1], B.J. Spillane, D.G. McGrath

[1]Rep. by J.J. Glennon

Tries: –
Cons: –
PG: Kiernan (2)
DG: –

P.H. Thorburn; I.C. Evans, J.A. Devereux, M.G. Ring, A.M. Hadley; J. Davies, R.N. Jones; J. Whitefoot, K. Phillips, S. Evans, *R.D. Moriarty, R.L. Norster, G.J. Roberts, W.P. Moriarty, R.G. Collins

Tries: Ring
Cons: –
PG: Thorburn
DG: Davies (2)

Referee: K.V.J. Fitzgerald (Australia)

WALES v. TONGA

Date: 29 May 1987   Venue: Showgrounds, Palmerston North
29–16

WALES	TONGA
2G, 2PG, 1DG, 2T	**1G, 2PG, 1T**

P.H. Thorburn; G.M.C. Webbe, M.G. Ring, K. Hopkins, A.M. Hadley; M. Dacey[2], R.N. Jones; †A. Buchanan, K. Phillips, S. Evans[1], *R.D. Moriarty, H.D. Richards, W.P. Moriarty, P.T. Davies, G.J. Roberts

[1]Rep. by S.W. Blackmore
[2]Rep. by J. Davies

Tries: Webbe (3), Hadley
Cons: Thorburn (2)
PG: Thorburn (2)
DG: J. Davies

T. Ete'aki; M. Vunipola, S. Mohi, T. Fukakitekei'aho, K. Fielea; A. 'Amone[2], T. Fifita; V. Lutua, A. Afu Fungavaka, H. Tupou[1], M. Tu'ungafasi, K. Fine, V. Tu'uta Kakato, M. Felise, *F. Valu

[1]Rep. by L. Va'Eno
[2]Rep. by A. Liava'a

Tries: Fielea, Fifita
Cons: Liava'a
PG: 'Amone, Liava'a
DG: –

Referee: D.J. Bishop (NZ)

IRELAND v. CANADA

Date: 30 May 1987 Venue: Carisbrook, Dunedin
46–19

IRELAND	**CANADA**
5G, 2DG, 2PG, 1T	4PG, 1DG, 1T

H.P. MacNeill; T.M. Ringland, B.J. Mullin, M.J. Kiernan, K.D. Crossan; A.J.P. Ward, M.T. Bradley; P.A. Orr, †J.P. McDonald, D.C. Fitzgerald, *D.G. Lenihan, W.A. Anderson, †P.C. Collins, B.J. Spillane, D.G. McGrath

M. Wyatt; P. Palmer, J. Lecky, S. McTavish, T. Woods; G. Rees, I. Stuart; E. Evans, M. Cardinal, W. Handson, R. Hindson, *H. de Goede, R. Frame, G. Ennis, R. Radu

Tries: Cardinal
Cons: –
PG: Rees (3), Wyatt
DG: Rees

Tries: Crossan (2), Bradley, Spillane, Ringland, MacNeill
Cons: Kiernan (5)
PG: Kiernan (2)
DG: Kiernan, Ward

Referee: F.A. Howard (England)

WALES v. CANADA

Date: 3 June 1987 Venue: Rugby Park, Invercargill
40–9

WALES	**CANADA**
4G, 4T	3PG

P.H. Thorburn; I.C. Evans, J.A. Devereux, B. Bowen[1], A.M. Hadley; *J. Davies, R. Giles; J. Whitefoot, A.J. Phillips, S.W. Blackmore, S. Sutton, R.L. Norster, W.P. Moriarty[2], P.T. Davies, G.J. Roberts

M. Wyatt; P. Palmer, T. Woods, J. Lecky, S. Gray; G. Rees, I. Stuart[1]; R. McKellar, K. Svoboda, W. Handson, R. Hindson, *H. de Goede, B. Breen, G. Ennis, R. Frame

[1]Rep. by D. Tucker

[1]Rep. by K. Hopkins
[2]Rep. by R.D. Moriarty

Tries: –
Cons: –
PG: Rees (3)
DG: –

Tries: Evans (4), Hadley, Phillips, Devereux, Bowen
Cons: Thorburn (4)
PG: –
DG: –

Referee: D.J. Bishop (NZ)

IRELAND v. TONGA

Date: 3 June 1987   Venue: Ballymore, Brisbane
32–9

IRELAND	**TONGA**
3G, 2PG, 2T	3PG

H.P. MacNeill; T.M. Ringland, B.J. Mullin, D.G. Irwin, K.D. Crossan; A.J.P. Ward, M.T. Bradley; †J.A. Langbroek, T. Kingston, J.J. McCoy, *D.G. Lenihan, W.A. Anderson, P.M. Matthews, †N. Francis, D.G. McGrath

T. Ete'aki; T. Fukakitekei'aho, A. Liava'a, S. Mohi, K. Fielea; A. Amone, T. Fifita; V. Lutua, A. Afu Fungavaka, H. Tupou, M. Tu'ungafasi, K. Fine, V. Tu'uta Kakato, M. Felise, *F. Valu

Tries: MacNeill (2), Mullin (3)   Tries: –
Cons: Ward (3)   Cons: –
PG: Ward (2)   PG: Amone (3)
DG: –   DG: –

Referee: G. Maurette (France)

OVERLEAF: Andy Earl charges through the Argentine defence with the great Hugo Porta in hot pursuit. Argentina were comprehensively beaten 46–15 in Wellington by a New Zealand side that included squad members who would not be seen in the World Cup final line up.

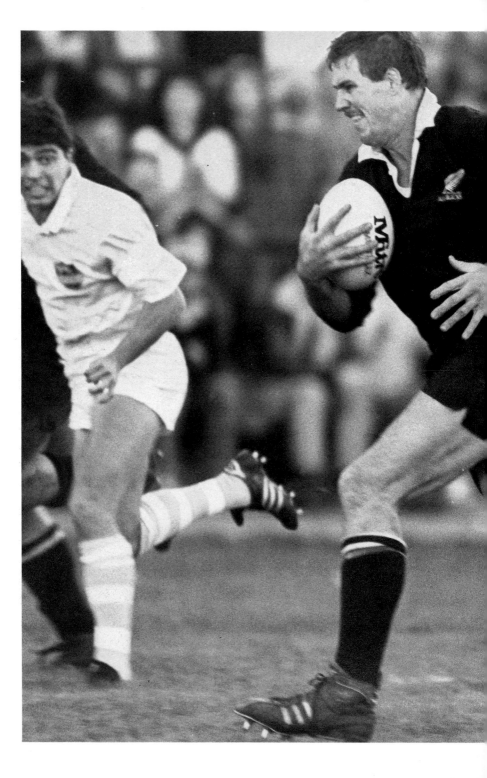

POOL THREE

	P	W	D	L	For	Against	Pts
New Zealand	3	3	0	0	190	34	6
Fiji	3	1	0	2	56	101	2
Argentina	3	1	0	2	49	90	2
Italy	3	1	0	2	40	110	2

NEW ZEALAND v. ITALY

Date: 22 May 1987   Venue: Eden Park, Auckland

70–6

NZ	**ITALY**
8G, 2PG, 4T	1PG, 1DG

†J.A. Gallagher; J.J. Kirwan, J.T. Stanley, W.T. Taylor, C.I. Green; G.J. Fox, *D.E. Kirk; †R.W. Loe, S.B.T Fitzpatrick, S.C. McDowell, M.J. Pierce, G.W. Whetton, A.J. Whetton, W.T. Shelford, †M.N. Jones

S. Ghizzoni; M. Mascioletti, F. Gaetaniello, O. Collodo, M. Cuttita; R. Ambrosio, F. Lorigiola; G. Rossi, G. Morelli, T. Lupini, F. Berni, M. Gardin, *M. Innocenti, G. Artuso, P. Farina

Tries: Jones, Kirk (2), Taylor, Green (2), Kirwan (2), McDowell, Stanley, Whetton (A.J.), Penalty try
Cons: Fox (8)
PG: Fox (2)
DG: –

Tries: –
Cons: –
PG: Collodo
DG: Collodo

Referee: R.J. Fordham (Australia)

FIJI v. ARGENTINA

Date: 24 May 1987   Venue: Rugby Park, Hamilton
28–9

FIJI
3G, 2PG, 1T

S. Koroduadua; K. Nalaga, T. Cama,
E. Naituku, S. Tuvula; E. Rokowailoa,
P. Tabulutu[1]; S. Naituku, S. Naiviliwasa,
R. Namoro, *K. Rakoroi, I. Savai, P. Gale[2],
J. Sanday, M. Qoro

[1]Rep. by P. Nawalu
[2]Rep. by S. Vunivalu

Tries: Gale, Rakoroi, Nalaga, Savai
Cons: Koroduadua (2), Rokowailoa
PG: Koroduadua (2)
DG: –

ARGENTINA
1G, 1PG

S. Salvat; M. Campo, D. Cuesta-Silva,
F. Turnes, J. Lanza; *H. Porta, F. Gomez;
F. Morel, D. Cash, L. Molina, E. Branca,
G. Milano[1], J. Allen, G. Travaglini, J. Mostany

[1]Rep. by A. Schiavio

Tries: Penalty try
Cons: Porta
PG: Porta
DG: –

Referee: J.M. Fleming (Scotland)

NEW ZEALAND v. FIJI

Date: 27 May 1987   Venue: Lancaster Park, Christchurch
74–13

NZ
10G, 2PG, 2T

J.A. Gallagher; J.J. Kirwan, J.T. Stanley,
W.T. Taylor, C.I. Green; G.J. Fox, *D.E. Kirk;
S.C. McDowell, S.B.T. Fitzpatrick, J.A. Drake,
A. Anderson, G.W. Whetton, A.J. Whetton,
W.T. Shelford, M.N. Jones

Tries: Green (4), Gallagher (4), Kirwan, Kirk,
  A. Whetton, Penalty try
Cons: Fox (10)
PG: Fox (2)
DG: –

FIJI
3PG, 1T

S. Koroduadua; T. Cama, S. Lovokuro,
J. Kubu, S. Tuvula; E. Rokowailoa, P. Nawalu;
P. Volavola, E. Rakai, M. Taga, J. Cama,
I. Savai, L. Kididromo, *K. Rakoroi,
S. Vunivalu

Tries: J. Cama
Cons: –
PG: Koroduadua (3)
DG: –

Referee: W.D. Bevan (Wales)

251

ARGENTINA v. ITALY

Date: 28 May 1987   Venue: Lancaster Park, Christchurch
25–16

ARGENTINA	ITALY
1G, 5PG, 1T	1G, 2PG, 1T

S. Salvat; J. Lanza, R. Madero, D. Cuesta-Silva, P. Lanza; *H. Porta, M. Yanguela[1]; S. Dengra, D. Cash, L. Molina, E. Branca, S. Carossio, J. Allen, G. Travaglini, A. Schlavio

[1]Rep. by F. Gomez

Tries: J. Lanza, Gomez
Cons: Porta
PG: Porta (5)
DG: –

D. Tebaldi; M. Mascioletti, F. Gaetaniello, S. Barba, M. Cuttita; O. Collodo, F. Lorigiola; G. Rossi, A. Galeazzo, T. Lupini, A. Colella, M. Gardin, M. Pavin, G. Zanon, *M. Innocenti

Tries: Cuttita, Innocenti
Cons: Collodo
PG: Collodo (2)
DG: –

Referee: R.C. Quittenton (England)

FIJI v. ITALY

Date: 31 May 1987   Venue: Carisbrook, Dunedin
15–18

FIJI	ITALY
1G, 1DG, 2PG	1PG, 1DG, 3T

S. Koroduadua; T. Cama, K. Salusalu, T. Mitchell, S. Tuvula[1]; E. Rokowailoa, P. Nawalu; S. Naituku, S. Naiviliwasa, P. Volavola, W. Nadolo, I. Savai, J. Sanday, *K. Rakoroi, M. Qoro

[1]Rep. by E. Naituku[2]
[2]Rep. by J. Kubu

Tries: Naiviliwasa
Cons: Koroduadua
PG: Koroduadua (2)
DG: Qoro

D. Tebaldi; M. Mascioletti, F. Gaetaniello, S. Barba, M. Cuttita; O. Collodo, A. Ghini; G. Cucchiella, S. Romagnoli, T. Lupini, M. Gardin, A. Colella, R. Dolfato, P. Farina, *M. Innocenti

Tries: Cuttita, Cucchiella, Mascioletti
Cons: –
PG: Collodo
DG: Collodo

Referee: K.H. Lawrence (NZ)

NEW ZEALAND v. ARGENTINA

Date: 1 June 1987   Venue: Athletic Park, Wellington
46–15

NZ	**ARGENTINA**
2G, 6PG, 4T	1G, 3PG

K.J. Crowley; J.J. Kirwan, J.T. Stanley, †B.J. McCahill, T.J. Wright; G.J. Fox, *D.E. Kirk; R.W. Loe, S.B.T. Fitzpatrick, J.A. Drake, M.J. Pierce, G.W. Whetton, A.J. Whetton, A.T. Earl, †M.Z. Brooke

G. Angaut; M. Campo, R. Madero, F. Turnes[1], J. Lanza; *H. Porta, F. Gomez; S. Dengra, D. Cash, L. Molina, E. Branca, S. Carossio, J. Allen, G. Travaglini[2], A. Schiavio

[1]Rep. by P. Lanza
[2]Rep. by J. Mostany

Tries: Kirk, Brooke, Stanley, Earl, Crowley, A. Whetton
Cons: Fox (2)
PG: Fox (6)
DG: –

Tries: J. Lanza
Cons: Porta
PG: Porta (3)
DG: –

Referee: R.C. Quittenton (England)

OVERLEAF: Australian prop Andy McIntyre is left on the ground as Phillipe Sella scores for France. This is one moment from arguably the greatest rugby game ever played; the 1987 World Cup semi-final clash which France won 30–24 with a late try from Serge Blanco.

POOL FOUR

	P	W	D	L	For	Against	Pts
France	3	2	1	0	145	44	5
Scotland	3	2	1	0	135	69	5
Romania	3	1	0	2	61	130	2
Zimbabwe	3	0	0	3	53	151	0

ROMANIA v. ZIMBABWE

Date: 23 May 1987   Venue: Eden Park, Auckland
21–20

ROMANIA
3PG, 3T

M. Toader; A. Marin[1], S. Tofan, A. Lungu,
V. David; D. Alexandru[2], *M. Paraschiv;
I. Bucan, E. Grigore, G. Leonte, L. Constantin,
S. Constantin, F. Murariu, C. Raducanu,
H. Dumitras

[1]Rep by L. Hodorca
[2]Rep by V. Ion

Tries: Paraschiv, Toader, Hodorca
Cons: –
PG: Alexandru (3)
DG: –

ZIMBABWE
1G, 2PG, 2T

A. Ferreira; P. Kaulbach, R. Tsimba[1],
K. Graham, E. Barrett; C. Brown, *M. Jellicoe;
G. Elcombe, L. Bray, A. Tucker, M. Sawyer,
M. Martin, R. Gray, M. Neill, D. Buitendag[2]

[1]Rep. by A. Buitendag
[2]Rep. by E. Bredenkamp

Tries: Tsimba (2), Neill
Cons: Ferreira
PG: Ferreira (2)
DG: –

Referee: S.R. Hilditch (Ireland)

FRANCE v. SCOTLAND

Date: 23 May 1987 Venue: Lancaster Park, Christchurch
20–20

FRANCE	SCOTLAND
1G, 2PG, 2T	4PG, 2T

S. Blanco; P. Lagisquet, P. Sella, D. Charvet, P. Esteve; F. Mesnel, P. Berbizier; P. Ondarts, *D. Dubroca, J-P. Garuet, A. Lorieux, J. Condom, E. Champ, L. Rodriguez, D. Erbani

A.G. Hastings; M.D.F. Duncan, K.W. Robertson, D.S. Wyllie, I. Tukalo; J.Y. Rutherford[1], R.J. Laidlaw; D.M.B. Sole, *C.T. Deans, I.G. Milne, D.B. White, A.J. Tomes, J. Jeffrey, I.A.M. Paxton, F. Calder

Tries: Sella, Berbizier, Blanco
Cons: Blanco
PG: Blanco (2)
DG: –

[1]Rep. by †A.V. Tait

Tries: White, Duncan
Cons: –
PG: Hastings (4)
DG: –

Referee: F.A. Howard (England)

FRANCE v. ROMANIA

Date: 28 May 1987 Venue: Athletic Park, Wellington
55–12

FRANCE	ROMANIA
8G, 1PG, 1T	4PG

S. Blanco[1]; P. Lagisquet, P. Sella, D. Charvet, M. Andrieu; G. Laporte, P. Berbizier; †L. Armary, *P. Dintrans, J-P. Garuet, F. Haget, J. Condom, E. Champ, D. Erbani, A. Carminati

V. Ion; M. Toader, S. Tofan, V. David, A. Lungu; R. Bezuscu, *M. Paraschiv; F. Opris, V. Ilca[1], V. Pascu, N. Veres, L. Constantin, E. Necula, C. Raducanu, G. Dumitru

[1]Rep. by D. Camberabero

[1]Rep. by E. Grigore

Tries: Lagisquet (2), Charvet (2), Sella, Andrieu, Camberabero, Erbani, Laporte
Cons: Laporte (8)
PG: Laporte
DG: –

Tries: –
Cons: –
PG: Bezuscu (4)
DG: –

Referee: R.J. Fordham (Australia)

SCOTLAND v. ZIMBABWE

Date: 30 May 1987   Venue: Athletic Park, Wellington

60–21

SCOTLAND	ZIMBABWE
8G, 3T	1G, 5PG

A.G. Hastings; M.D.F. Duncan, A.V. Tait, K.W. Robertson, I. Tukalo; D.S. Wyllie, †G.H. Oliver; D.M.B. Sole, *C.T. Deans, I.G. Milne, J.R.E. Campbell-Lamerton, A.J. Tomes, J. Jeffrey, I.A.M. Paxton, F. Calder

A. Ferreira; S. Graham, A. Buitendag, K. Graham, E. Barrett; M. Grobler, *M. Jellicoe; A. Nicholls, L. Bray, A. Tucker, M. Sawyer, M. Martin, R. Gray, M. Neill, D. Buitendag

Tries: Tait (2), Duncan (2), Tukalo (2), Paxton (2), Oliver, Hastings, Jeffrey
Cons: Hastings (8)
PG: –
DG: –

Tries: D. Buitendag
Cons: Grobler
PG: Grobler (5)
DG: –

Referee: D.I.H. Burnett (Ireland)

FRANCE v. ZIMBABWE

Date: 2 June 1987   Venue: Eden Park, Auckland

70–12

FRANCE	ZIMBABWE
9G, 4T	1G, 2PG

D. Camberabero; M. Andrieu, E. Bonneval[1], D. Charvet, P. Esteve; F. Mesnel, †R. Modin; †J.L. Tolot, *D. Dubroca, P. Ondarts, A. Lorieux, J. Condom, A. Carminati, L. Rodriguez, J.L. Joinel;

A. Ferreira; P. Kaulbach, R. Tsimba, K. Graham, E. Barrett; M. Grobler, *M. Jellicoe; G. Elcombe[1], L. Bray, A. Tucker, M. Sawyer, M. Martin[2], R. Gray, M. Neill, D. Buitendag

[1]Rep. by P. Sella[2]
[2]Rep. by G. Laporte

[1]Rep. by A. Nicholls
[2]Rep. by N. Kloppers

Tries: Modin (3), Camberabero (3), Charvet (2), Dubroca, Esteve, Rodriguez (2), Laporte
Cons: Camberabero (9)
PG: –
DG: –

Tries: Kaulbach
Cons: Grobler
PG: Grobler (2)
DG: –

Referee: W.D. Bevan (Wales)

SCOTLAND v. ROMANIA

Date: 2 June 1987   Venue: Carisbrook, Dunedin
55–28

SCOTLAND	ROMANIA
8G, 1PG, 1T	2G, 4PG, 1T

A.G. Hastings; M.D.F. Duncan, A.V. Tait,
S. Hastings[1], I. Tukalo; D.S. Wyllie,
R.J. Laidlaw; D.M.B. Sole, *C.T. Deans,
N.A. Rowan, D.B. White, A.J. Tomes[2],
J. Jeffrey, I.A.M. Paxton, F. Calder

A. Ion; A. Pilotschi, A. Lungu, S. Tofan,
M. Toader; D. Alexandru, *M. Paraschiv;
I. Bucan, E. Grigore, G. Leonte, S. Constantin,
L. Constantin, F. Murariu, C. Raducanu[1],
H. Dumitras

[1]Rep. by †R. Cramb
[2]Rep. by J.R.E. Campbell-Lamerton

[1]Rep. by G. Dumitru

Tries: Tait (2), A.G. Hastings (2), Jeffrey (3),
    Duncan, Tukalo
Cons: A.G. Hastings (8)
PG: A.G. Hastings
DG: –

Tries: Murariu (2), Toader
Cons: Alexandru, Ion
PG: Alexandru (3), Ion
DG: –

Referee: S.R. Hilditch (Ireland)

KNOCKOUT ROUNDS
QUARTER FINALS

NEW ZEALAND v. SCOTLAND

Date: 6 June 1987   Venue: Lancaster Park, Christchurch
30–3

NZ	SCOTLAND
2G, 6PG	1PG

J.A. Gallagher; J.J. Kirwan, J.T. Stanley, W.T. Taylor[1], C.I. Green; G.J. Fox, *D.E. Kirk; S.C. McDowell, S.B.T. Fitzpatrick, J.A. Drake, M.J. Pierce, G.W. Whetton, A.J. Whetton, W.T. Shelford, M.N. Jones	A.G. Hastings; M.D.F. Duncan, A.V. Tait, K.W. Robertson, I. Tukalo; D.S. Wyllie, R.J. Laidlaw; D.M.B. Sole, *C.T. Deans, I.G. Milne, D.B. White, A.J. Tomes, †D.J. Turnbull, I.A.M Paxton, F. Calder

[1]Rep by B.J. McCahill

Tries: A.J. Whetton, Gallagher
Cons: Fox (2)
PG: Fox (6)
DG: –

Tries: –
Cons: –
PG: Hastings
DG: –

Referee: D.I.H. Burnett (Ireland)

Concentration is etched on the face of Wade Dooley, England's most capped lock-forward, at a line out against Wales. Dooley has developed into one of rugby's great ball winning forwards in the mayhem that constitutes international line outs. He plays for Preston Grasshoppers, one of English rugby's less glamorous teams.

FRANCE v. FIJI

Date: 7 June 1987   Venue: Eden Park, Auckland
31–16

FRANCE	FIJI
3G, 2PG, 1DG, 1T	1G, 2PG, 1T

S. Blanco[1]; D. Charvet, P. Sella, F. Mesnel,	J. Kubu; J. Damu, K. Salusalu, T. Cama,
P. Lagisquet; G. Laporte, P. Berbizier;	T. Mitchell; S. Koroduadua, P. Nawalu;
P. Ondarts, *D. Dubroca, J-P. Garuet,	R. Namoro, E. Rakai, S. Naituku, *K. Rakoroi,
F. Haget, A. Lorieux, E. Champ, L. Rodriguez,	I. Savai[2], M. Qoro[1], L. Kididromo,
D. Erbani	S. Naiviliwasa

[1]Rep. by D. Camberabero	[1]Rep. by S.Vunivalu
	[2]Rep. by W. Nadolo
Tries: Rodriguez (2), Lorieux, Lagisquet	
Cons: Laporte (3)	Tries: Qoro, Damu
PG: Laporte (2)	Cons: Koroduadua
DG: Laporte	PG: Koroduadua (2)
	DG: –

Referee: C. Norling (Wales)

AUSTRALIA v. IRELAND

Date: 7 June 1987   Venue: Concord Oval, Sydney
33–15

AUSTRALIA	IRELAND
4G, 3PG	2G, 1PG

D.I. Campese; P.C. Grigg, *A.G. Slack,	H.P. MacNeill; T.M. Ringland, B.J. Mullin[2],
B. Papworth, M.P. Burke; M.P. Lynagh,	M.J. Kiernan, K.D. Crossan; P.M. Dean,
N.C. Farr-Jones[1]; C.A. Lillicrap, T.A. Lawton,	M.T. Bradley; P.A. Orr, T. Kingston,
A.J. McIntyre, S.A.G. Cutler, W.A. Campbell,	D.C. Fitzgerald, *D.G. Lenihan,
S.P. Poidevin, S.N. Tuynman, J.S. Miller	W.A. Anderson, P.M. Matthews, N. Francis[1],
	D.G. McGrath

[1]Rep. by B. Smith	
	[1]Rep. by B.J. Spillane
Tries: Smith, McIntyre, Burke (2)	[2]Rep. by D.G. Irwin
Cons: Lynagh (4)	
PG: Lynagh (3)	Tries: MacNeill, Kiernan
DG: –	Cons: Kiernan (2)
	PG: Kiernan
	DG: –

Referee: J.B. Anderson (Scotland)

WALES v. ENGLAND

Date: 8 June 1987   Venue: Ballymore, Brisbane
16–3

WALES	ENGLAND
2G, 1T	1PG

P.H. Thorburn; I.C. Evans, J.A. Devereux,
B. Bowen, A.M. Hadley; J. Davies,
R.N. Jones; A. Buchanan, A.J. Phillips,
†D. Young, *R.D. Moriarty, R.L. Norster[1],
G.J. Roberts, W.P. Moriarty, R.G. Collins

J. Webb; *M.E. Harrison, K.G. Simms,
J.L.B. Salmon, R. Underwood; P.N. Williams,
R.M. Harding; P.A.G. Rendall[1], B.C. Moore,
G.S. Pearce, W.A. Dooley, N.C. Redman,
P.J. Winterbottom, D. Richards, G.W. Rees

[1]Rep. by H.D. Richards

[1]Rep. by G.J. Chilcott

Tries: Roberts, Jones, Devereux
Cons: Thorburn (2)
PG: –
DG: –

Tries: –
Cons: –
PG: Webb
DG: –

Referee: R. Hourquet (France)

SEMI-FINALS

FRANCE v. AUSTRALIA

Date: 13 June 1987 Venue: Concord Oval, Sydney

30–24

FRANCE	AUSTRALIA
4G, 2PG	2G, 1DG, 3PG

S. Blanco; D. Camberabero, P. Sella,
D. Charvet, P. Lagisquet; F. Mesnel,
P. Berbizier; P. Ondarts, *D. Dubroca,
J-P. Garuet, A. Lorieux, J. Condom,
E. Champ, L. Rodriguez, D. Erbani

Tries: Lorieux, Lagisquet, Sella, Blanco
Cons: Camberabero (4)
PG: Camberabero (2)
DG: –

D.I. Campese; P.C. Grigg, *A.G. Slack,
B. Papworth[1], M. Burke; M.P. Lynagh,
N.C. Farr-Jones; C.A. Lillicrap, T.A. Lawton,
A.J. McIntyre, S.A.G. Cutler, W.A. Campbell[2],
S.P. Poidevin, T. Coker, J.S. Miller

[1]Rep. by A. Herbert
[2]Rep. by D. Codey

Tries: Campese, Codey
Cons: Lynagh (2)
PG: Lynagh (3)
DG: Lynagh

Referee: J.B. Anderson (Scotland)

WALES v. NEW ZEALAND

Date: 14 June 1987 Venue: Ballymore, Brisbane
6–49

WALES	NEW ZEALAND
1G	7G, 1PG, 1T

P.H. Thorburn; I.C. Evans, J.A. Devereux, B. Bowen, A.M. Hadley; J. Davies, R.N. Jones; A. Buchanan, K. Phillips, D. Young, *R.D. Moriarty, H.D. Richards, W.P. Moriarty, P.T. Davies, R.G. Collins[1]

J.A. Gallagher; J.J. Kirwan, J.T. Stanley[1], W.T. Taylor, C.I. Green; G.J. Fox, *D.E. Kirk; S.C. McDowell, S.B.T. Fitzpatrick, J.A. Drake, M.J. Pierce, G.W. Whetton, A.J. Whetton, W.T. Shelford, M. Brooke-Cowden

[1]Rep. by S. Sutton

[1]Rep. by B.J. McCahill

Tries: Devereux
Cons: Thorburn
PG: –
DG: –

Tries: Kirwan (2), Stanley, Drake, A. Whetton, Shelford (2), Brooke-Cowden
Cons: Fox (7)
PG: Fox
DG: –

Referee: K.V.J. Fitzgerald (Australia)

THIRD/FOURTH PLACE PLAYOFF MATCH

AUSTRALIA v. WALES

Date: 18 June 1987   Venue: International Park, Rotorua
21–22

AUSTRALIA	WALES
2G, 2PG, 1DG	2G, 2PG, 1T

A. Leeds; P.C. Grigg[1], *A.G. Slack,
M.P. Burke, D.I. Campese; M.P. Lynagh,
B. Smith; C.A. Lillicrap[2], T.A. Lawton,
A.J. McIntyre, S.A.G. Cutler, T. Coker,
S.P. Poidevin, S.N. Tuynman, D. Codey

P.H. Thorburn; I.C. Evans, J.A. Devereux,
M.G. Ring, A.M. Hadley; J. Davies,
R.N. Jones; A. Buchanan, A.J. Phillips,
S.W. Blackmore, *R.D. Moriarty, S. Sutton,
G.J. Roberts, W.P. Moriarty, †R. Webster

[1]Rep. by N.C. Farr-Jones
[2]Rep. by E.E. Rodriguez

Tries: Roberts, W.P. Moriarty, Hadley
Cons: Thorburn (2)
PG: Thorburn (2)
DG: –

Tries: Burke, Grigg
Cons: Lynagh (2)
PG: Lynagh (2)
DG: Lynagh

Referee: F.A. Howard (England)

THE FINAL

NEW ZEALAND v. FRANCE

Date: 20 June 1987   Venue: Eden Park, Auckland
29–9

NEW ZEALAND	FRANCE
1G, 1DG, 4PG, 2T	1G, 1PG

J.A. Gallagher; J.J. Kirwan, J.T. Stanley,
W.T. Taylor, C.I. Green; G.J. Fox, *D.E. Kirk;
S.C. McDowell, S.B.T. Fitzpatrick, J.A. Drake,
M.J. Pierce, G.W. Whetton, A.J. Whetton,
W.T. Shelford, M.N. Jones

S. Blanco; D. Camberabero, P. Sella,
D. Charvet, P. Lagisquet; F. Mesnel,
P. Berbizier; P. Ondarts, *D. Dubroca,
J-P. Garuet, A. Lorieux, J. Condom,
E. Champ, L. Rodriguez, D. Erbani

Tries: Kirwan, Jones, Kirk
Cons: Fox
PG: Fox (4)
DG: Fox

Tries: Berbizier
Cons: Camberabero
PG: Camberabero
DG: –

Referee: K.V.J. Fitzgerald (Australia)

WORLD RECORDS OF MAJOR INTERNATIONAL MATCHES

(up to 31 March 1991)

Major international records cover performances by teams and players of full member Unions of the International Board, Test matches played by the Lions, and matches staged during the World Cup tournament in 1987.

CAREER RECORDS

(official Tests for Lions included)

Most Appearances in Major Internationals

85	S Blanco	France
81	C M H Gibson	Ireland/Lions
80	W J McBride	Ireland/Lions
72	P Sella	France
69	R Bertranne	France
65	J F Slattery	Ireland/Lions
63	G O Edwards	Wales/Lions
63	J P R Williams	Wales/Lions
63	M Crauste	France
63	B Dauga	France
61	J Condom	France
60	A R Irvine	Scotland/Lions

Most Points in Major Internationals

564	M P Lynagh	Australia
430	G J Fox	New Zealand
329	A G Hastings	Scotland/Lions
308	M J Kiernan	Ireland/Lions
301	A R Irvine	Scotland/Lions
301	P H Thorburn	Wales
268	H E Botha	South Africa
265	J-P Romeu	France
260	P E McLean	Australia
254	D Camberabero	France
243	S O Campbell	Ireland/Lions
240	W H Hare	England

Most Consecutive Appearances for a Nation in Major Internationals

53	G O Edwards	Wales
52	W J McBride	Ireland
49	A B Carmichael	Scotland
49	P A Orr	Ireland

Most Tries in Major Internationals

37	D I Campese	Australia
33	S Blanco	France
28	J J Kirwan	New Zealand
27	R Underwood	England/Lions
24	I S Smith	Scotland/Lions
23	C Darrouy	France
23	T G R Davies	Wales/Lions
23	P Sella	France
20	G O Edwards	Wales/Lions
20	P Lagisquet	France

Most Appearances as Captain in Major Internationals

34	J-P Rives	France
30	W J Whineray	New Zealand
28	T J Kiernan	Ireland/Lions
25	W B Beaumont	England/Lions

Most Conversions in Major Internationals

97	M P Lynagh	Australia
90	G J Fox	New Zealand
47	A G Hastings	Scotland/Lions
45	M Vannier	France
43	H E Botha	South Africa
43	P H Thorburn	Wales
40	M J Kiernan	Ireland/Lions
38	J Bancroft	Wales

Most Penalty Goals in Major Internationals

105	M P Lynagh	Australia
76	G J Fox	New Zealand
69	P H Thorburn	Wales
67	A R Irvine	Scotland/Lions
67	W H Hare	England
65	A G Hastings	Scotland/Lions
62	M J Kiernan	Ireland/Lions
62	P E McLean	Australia
61	S O Campbell	Ireland/Lions
56	J-P Romeu	France

Most Dropped Goals in Major Internationals

15	J-P Lescarboura	France	11	C R Andrew	England/Lions
15	H E Botha	South Africa	10	B John	Wales/Lions
13	J Davies	Wales	10	D Camberabero	France
12	P Albaladejo	France	9	P F Hawthorne	Australia
12	J Y Rutherford	Scotland/Lions	9	J-P Romeu	France
11	G Camberabero	France	9	M P Lynagh	Australia

Most Points in a Match

By a team

74	New Zealand v Fiji	Christchurch	1987
70	New Zealand v Italy	Auckland	1987
70	France v Zimbabwe	Auckland	1987
67	Australia v United States	Brisbane	1990
65	Australia v South Korea	Brisbane	1987
60	France v Italy	Toulon	1967
60	Ireland v Romania	Dublin	1986
60	England v Japan	Sydney	1987
60	Scotland v Zimbabwe	Wellington	1987
60	New Zealand v Argentina	Dunedin	1989

By a player

30	D Camberabero	France v Zimbabwe	1987
27	G Camberabero	France v Italy	1967
27	A G Hastings	Scotland v Romania	1987
26	A R Hewson	New Zealand v Australia	1982
26	G J Fox	New Zealand v Fiji	1987
25	J-P Romeu	France v United States	1976
25	P Berot	France v Romania	1987

Most Tries in a Match

By a team

13	England v Wales	Blackheath	1881
13	New Zealand v United States	Berkeley	1913
13	France v Romania	Paris	1924
13	Australia v South Korea	Brisbane	1987
13	France v Zimbabwe	Auckland	1987
12	Scotland v Wales	Edinburgh	1887
12	New Zealand v Italy	Auckland	1987
12	New Zealand v Fiji	Christchurch	1987
12	Australia v United States	Brisbane	1990

By a player

5	G C Lindsay	Scotland v Wales	1887
5	D Lambert	England v France	1907
5	R Underwood	England v Fiji	1989

Most Conversions in a Match

By a team

10	New Zealand v Fiji	Christchurch	1987
9	France v Italy	Toulon	1967
9	France v Zimbabwe	Auckland	1987

By a player

10	G J Fox	New Zealand v Fiji	1987
9	G Camberabero	France v Italy	1967
9	D Camberabero	France v Zimbabwe	1987

Most Penalty Goals in a Match

By a team

7	South Africa v France	Pretoria	1975
7	England v Wales	Cardiff	1991

By a player

7	S D Hodgkinson	England v Wales	1991

MATCH RECORDS

Most Consecutive Matches Won

17	by New Zealand	1965–69
12	by New Zealand	1988–90
11	by Wales	1907–10

Most Consecutive Matches Without Defeat

23	by New Zealand	1987–90
17	by New Zealand	1961–64
17	by New Zealand	1965–69

FOLLOW THE 1991 WORLD CUP: YOUR GAME BY GAME RECORD

DATE	POOL	GAME	TIME	VENUE	RESULT
Oct 3	1	England v New Zealand	3pm	Twickenham	12 – 18
Oct 4	3	Australia v Argentina	3pm	Llanelli	32 – 19
Oct 4	4	France v Romania	8pm	Beziers	30 – 3
Oct 5	1	Italy v USA	1pm	Otley	30 – 9
Oct 5	2	Scotland v Japan	3pm	Murrayfield	47 – 9
Oct 5	4	Fiji v Canada	8pm	Bayonne	3 – 16
Oct 6	3	Wales v Western Samoa	1pm	Cardiff	13 – 16
Oct 6	2	Ireland v Zimbabwe	3pm	Dublin	55 – 11
Oct 8	1	New Zealand v USA	1pm	Gloucester	46 – 6
Oct 8	1	England v Italy	3pm	Twickenham	36 – 6
Oct 8	4	France v Fiji	8pm	Grenoble	33 – 9
Oct 9	3	Australia v Western Samoa	1pm	Pontypool	9 – 3
Oct 9	2	Ireland v Japan	3pm	Dublin	32 – 16
Oct 9	2	Scotland v Zimbabwe	3pm	Murrayfield	51 – 12
Oct 9	3	Wales v Argentina	8pm	Cardiff	16 – 7
Oct 9	4	Canada v Romania	8pm	Toulouse	19 – 11
Oct 11	1	England v USA	3pm	Twickenham	37 – 9
Oct 12	2	Scotland v Ireland	1.30pm	Murrayfield	
Oct 12	3	Wales v Australia	3.15pm	Cardiff	
Oct 12	4	Fiji v Romania	7pm	Brive	
Oct 13	3	Argentina v Western Samoa	1pm	Pontypridd	
Oct 13	1	New Zealand v Italy	3pm	Leicester	
Oct 13	4	France v Canada	8pm	Agen	
Oct 14	2	Zimbabwe v Japan	3pm	Belfast	
Oct 19	C	Winner Pool 2 v R.Up Pool 3	1pm	Murrayfield	
Oct 19	B	Winner Pool 4 v R.Up Pool 2	3pm	Paris	
Oct 20	D	Winner Pool 3 v R.Up Pool 2	1pm	Dublin	
Oct 20	A	Winner Pool 1 v R.Up Pool 4	3pm	Lille	
Oct 26	Semi-final B v C	England 's Scotland	2.30pm	Murrayfield	9 – 6
Oct 27	Semi-final A v D		2.30pm	Dublin	16 – 6
Oct 30	Play-Off	NZ Australia vs New Zealand vs Scotland	2.30pm	Cardiff	
Nov 2	FINAL	England	2.30pm	Twickenham	12 – 6

(*LOCAL)

HOW THE 1991 WORLD CUP POOLS FINISHED

Pool 1

		P	W	D	L	Pts
1	New Zealand	3	3	0	0	9
2	England	3	2	0	1	6
3	Italy	3	1	0	2	3
4	USA	3	0	3	0	0

Pool 2

		P	W	D	L	Pts
1	Scotland	3	3	0	0	9
4	Japan	3	0	0	3	3
2	Ireland	3	2	0	1	6
3	Zimbabwe	3	0	0	3	3

Pool 3

		P	W	D	L	Pts
1	Australia	3	3	0	0	9
2	Argentina	3	1	0	2	3
4	Wales	3	0	0	3	0
3	Western Samoa	3	2	0	1	6

Pool 4

		P	W	D	L	Pts
3	Canada	3	2	0	1	6
4	Romania	3	1	0	2	3
2	Fiji	3	0	0	3	0
1	France	3	3	0	0	9

Quarter-final Results

France v England

Australia 19 v Ireland 18

Scotland v W. Samoa

New Zealand v Canada

Semi-final Results

A Scotland 6 vB England 9

B New Zealand 6 vC Australia 16

Final

England 6 v Australia 12

Winner 1991

Australia

272